MULTI-AGE

GROUPINGS

IN THE EARLY YEARS

Linda Hart-Hewins/Una Villiers

Pembroke Publishers Limited

*To our friendship of more than thirty years
and our friendship in the future*

© 1997 Pembroke Publishers Limited
538 Hood Road
Markham, Ontario L3R 3K9 Canada

Canadian Cataloguing in Publication Data

Hart-Hewins, Linda
    Multi-age groupings

Includes index.
ISBN 1-55138-042-0

1. Classroom learning centers. 2. Nongraded schools. 3.
Education, Primary. I. Villiers, Una. II. Title.

LB3044.8.H37 1997   372.13'078   C96-932385-9

Editor: Kate Revington
Design: John Zehethofer
Typesetting: Jay Tee Graphics Ltd.

Printed and bound in Canada
9 8 7 6 5 4 3 2 1

Contents

1/What Is a Multi-Age Grouping?

Misconceptions About the Phenomenon

In our work with teachers, parents, administrators, and concerned taxpayers we are constantly asked, "What is this strange thing called multi-age grouping?" Questions such as "How will my child learn in this kind of organization? What are the benefits? How can one teacher cope with all the different levels of ability and curricular demands?" are common.

People are confused about multi-age groupings. Often, their own educational experiences have not included such organizations. For many, the phenomenon is unfamiliar. Many parents have had other schooling experiences, such as split grades or one-room schools. Although these programs have more than one age in them, they are quite different from the multi-age grouping (MAG) programs that we advocate. In split grades, the teacher teaches the children in two distinct groups which are determined by age and grade. In a one-room school the teacher also teaches to the age and grade of the children. In multi-age grouping classrooms, teachers view the learning experiences differently. They group the children according to their developmental levels regardless of their age and grade. There are two or more grade levels in the classroom.

Parents generally suffer from misgivings about any multi-age grouping. They don't understand it, can't possibly imagine its benefits, and fear that their children's learning and academic progress will suffer if they are part of such a classroom organization — they don't want to see their children become what appear to be guinea pigs.

We decided to write this book to help clear up some of the misconceptions held by the public as well as by educators. As enthusiastic advocates for multi-age groupings, we are disturbed that many educators and the public hold these myths and misconceptions. Some of them are outlined below:

- the older children will regress or be held back by the younger children;
- the younger children will feel pressured to achieve the standards of the older children;
- teachers will be unable to provide a challenging and supportive program for such a wide range of abilities;
- the children will become bored if they are with the same teacher for more than one year;
- the children will have to stay for a longer period of time with one teacher and one group of children even if their situation is unsatisfactory.

We are also concerned that many teachers face the prospect of teaching MAG classrooms ill prepared and lacking in desire and practical experience to do so. Few resources have been available to help new MAG teachers begin. We will, therefore, devote the major portion of this book to a description of the practicalities of implementing such a program. We will also address specifics of timetabling, necessary learning centres, the role of the teacher, authentic assessment and evaluation techniques, and major parent concerns.

In this book, we want to share our enthusiasm for multi-age groupings, particularly in the early years (Junior Kindergarten to Grade 3). We also hope to help teachers of young children understand the benefits and practicalities of how to manage and operate within such an organization. We will share the insights, strategies, and resources that we have acquired throughout our teaching careers. Chapter 2 will look at the advantages of multi-age groupings.

Our Search for a New Model

After working in a variety of roles, consulting and administrating, we both agree that we are most enthusiastic about those years in which we taught in MAG settings.

Such an organization seemed to flow naturally from our common understandings and beliefs about how young children learn. We believe that learning is developmental, active, integrated, collaborative, continuous and socially interactive. These characteristics are all true of multi-age groupings.

The traditional organization by age does not seem to provide sufficient time or opportunities for such learning to occur. Also, its automatic transfer of students to a new classroom and teacher at the end of each school year frustrated us. Just when we were beginning to know our children, their families, and their needs, they were uprooted and transferred to another environment with different classmates, a new teacher and new expectations. Surely another model would avoid this.

In the early 1970s our study of the British Infant Schools, where each five-year-old was matched with a relative, friend, or volunteer in a multi-age, or family, grouping, offered us another model of classroom organization. We adapted this model to create *our* model of a multi-age grouping.

How We Began

We first sought administrative approval for a two-year implementation of a class with three grades/ages. We developed an inclusionary model with the following criteria for admission: parental approval, a representative range of abilities, and a balance of boys, girls, and second language learners. Other considerations included place in the family, the needs of only children and the presence in the classroom of siblings or friends. We met with the parents and shared with them the history and current research about multi-age groupings. We outlined our goals for the future, as well as our methods of evaluation, and asked for their support. Parents and both principals agreed to begin the project. No children were admitted to the program without their parents' approval and support.

In the first year of the project most parents felt comfortable with a Junior Kindergarten/Kindergarten combination. We kept a group of our JK students (approximately 50 percent) for Senior Kindergarten and registered new JK children. The class size was approximately fifty children — twenty-five in the morning and twenty-five in the afternoon. In the second year of the project some parents felt apprehensive about their children remaining for Grade 1. However, other parents felt confident and entrusted their children for another year. Predictably, these parents became our best advocates, and the popularity of the program increased by word of mouth. At the same time, other teachers were questioning the traditional organization and experimenting with similar MAG classrooms.

After the initial year, our numbers increased to thirty each morning and afternoon; we both had long waiting lists of parents who wanted their children to participate in this learning experience. From then on, parents felt confident and adamant that these classrooms would continue. And since their initiation, these two MAG classrooms have continued, despite the fact that the teachers, parents and children have changed.

Today, in the city of Toronto, most Kindergarten classrooms are organized in a MAG fashion and some include Grade 1. A Senior Kindergarten/Grade 1/Grade 2 combination is another popular model as is a Grade 1/2/3. However many of these combinations are treated by the teacher as if they were split grades. Beyond Grade 3, the number of MAG classrooms seems to decrease as teachers become less child focused and more content- and skills-driven according to age and grade.

Some educators believe that the move to outcome-based education inhibits multi-age groupings. However we believe that MAG organizations afford children a more flexible time frame to achieve the desired outcomes. The flexibility of organization in MAG settings affords students the appropriate amount of time and opportunity to succeed. Some children will need more time than others.

Varying Reasons for MAG Classrooms

We introduced MAG classrooms for positive reasons based on research. More recently, however, it seems that there are many different reasons for school boards to organize schools more creatively. Budgetary constraints, declining enrolments, increased research around the relationship between learning and teaching, and a belief by some educators that a multi-age experience is more advantageous for children are but a few of these divergent reasons.

Classrooms with two- or three-year grade/age spans are becoming more and more common, but they are all very different! Although they often use the same labels — vertical grouping, multi-age grouping, family grouping, heterogeneous grouping or non-graded — they are created for different reasons. Therefore, questions about multi-age groupings have no one answer. The answers depend very much on the reasons for creating such organizations.

A Family Grouping

Our intention is to answer these questions in the context of our own vision and experience of what MAG classrooms are and are not. Central to this is a belief in the multi-age grouping as a "family grouping." As advocates of multi-age grouping, we often use the term "family grouping" interchangeably with "multi-age grouping." "Family grouping" may better describe what actually occurs within our classes. **The very best of family components are incorporated into the school setting, helping, in our opinion, to ensure a more successful learning experience for young children.** These components include

- the diverse age of the members,
- the necessary presence of a wide range of tasks that need to be accomplished,
- many natural opportunities for assuming responsibility,

- the presence of a cooperative, collaborative spirit and a feeling of togetherness,
- the support of many competent guides and helpers,
- the expectation and acceptance of diversity, and
- the formation of long-term close relationships.

Although the term "multi-age" alone does not capture the essence of the atmosphere and organization in our heterogeneously grouped settings, it is a term that the public can readily understand and identify with. For us, these organizations are much more than "the putting together" of children of several ages. They reflect the very best of family life, which helps the learning process. To simply put children of different ages together is not enough. It is essential to re-create the successful conditions of a family setting.

How Multi-Age Groupings Should Work

Multi-age grouping is a school organization that resembles the structure of a family. There are different ages of children who may spend up to three years with the same teacher and a core group of their peers. Ideally, there is a balanced combination of age, ability, ethnicity and gender. Each year the oldest children exit, and a new group of beginners enter. Selections for entry or exit are not determined by a particular level of ability. Rather, they are determined by a variety of other factors which include parental support for the program, place in the family, and the presence of friends or siblings.

Unlike a family, if conflicts arise children are not limited to one teacher for an extended period of time. Parents are reassured that should conflicts arise, students are free to change classrooms at the end of each school year. During the school year, other problems of placement, such as personality or peer conflicts, are treated in the same manner as in grade by grade organizations. Decisions regarding placement always involve discussions with the parents.

The MAG teacher plans opportunities for students of several ages to learn together. The students can thereby spark

and support each other's thinking, acquisition, and consolidation of learning and growth. Strategies such as peer coaching and tutoring are encouraged, modelled, valued and used to help realize this.

The teacher takes a multi-faceted teaching approach, providing many activities and tasks which offer a wide range of opportunities for success at a variety of levels. The teacher plans for these activities to occur simultaneously and creates a timetable that provides large blocks of time in which children can work together.

As a coach, resource, facilitator and instructor moving from group to group, from student to student, the teacher seldom decides that the whole class will engage in the same task at the same time. Large group activities such as singing, drama and storytelling are carefully planned. Rarely the children do identical tasks. When the teacher does plan such activities, he or she actively considers children's interests, attention spans, and the learning purposes of the activities. For example, all the children might be required to do a page for a whole class book.

The teacher views the children as partners in this learning. The responsibility for choice and the direction the learning takes are shared. The extended period of time that the children and teacher spend together permits strong relationships to be formed between the children, the children and their teacher, and the teacher and the children's families.

2/Advantages of MAG Classrooms

Differences Between MAG and Single-Grade Classrooms

At a quick glance, if you had peered into our MAG classrooms, you would have thought that they looked the same as many single-grade rooms that have a developmental philosophy of learning. The only visible difference would have been the presence of different sizes of furniture, although even this fact would be true of many single-grade classrooms where teachers provide furniture to meet the different physical characteristics of the children.

We expected, as we went along with our original MAG project, to make significant changes to accommodate the three-age span. Experience, however, did not bear this out. Rather, it proved to be a matter of building and expanding upon what we already practised.

Some aspects were the same, others different. We still had permanent and temporary learning centres. The timetable was essentially the same. The role of the teacher, though, became more complex. The students were more involved in the daily running of the classroom, in accepting responsibility for their own learning, and in helping and supporting each other's learning. We rejected prepackaged curricula and lecture-style formats, where the teacher was perceived to know all the answers, in favor of curricula designed to fit the students' varying needs, interests and abilities.

The curricula changed from year to year as the group's needs changed. We continued to have high expectations for all our students in the Arts, Language, Math/Science/Technology, and Personal and Social Studies. Over time, however, we gained confidence in the ability of the children to pursue personal and group challenges or projects for their learning that surpassed our expectations. **They wrote more, they read more, and they initiated more personal inquiries than we had ever observed in a single-grade/age classroom.**

The Major Types of Advantages

We believe that our model of multi-age grouping has many advantages.

Research has shown that the most significant advantages are in the affective, or emotional, domain. The 1991 Canadian Education Association publication, *The Multi-Grade Classroom: Myth and Reality*, reflects this. It highlights the following benefit: "The specific traits that researchers have isolated as comparable or superior are independence, dependability, confidence, responsibility, cooperation with others, interaction skills, social skills, study habits and attitudes towards school."

The Building of Self-Confidence

For us, the key advantage is the building of self-confidence in learners.

In a MAG classroom, children have many natural opportunities to develop a strong sense of themselves as learners. Just as in a family, with a variety of ages and abilities, each member of the group is expected to have different skills, knowledge, attitudes and interests; to share and to help others; and to work and learn with others. Learners expect to be different and understand that all individuals do not possess the same skills.

We find that children in such a learning organization are more willing to take risks. They understand that their efforts will be accepted and supported rather than compared and contrasted to peers of the same age. In such an atmosphere of acceptance, where diversity is celebrated, self-confidence is boosted.

Although children can gain self-confidence in single-age classrooms with a similar philosophy of learning, MAG classes are more conducive to this. They offer more natural opportunities for building confidence. Because the children's ages differ, teachers cannot hold similar expectations for all the children, something that some teachers in single-grade classrooms are tempted to do. These teachers are often constrained by age and grade expectations to create similar learning experiences and expectations for all children. Teachers in MAG classrooms, however, are released from the constraints of single-age/grade expectations. Just as parents in a family expect differences among their children, they are free to expect, value, and capitalize on the wide range of abilities, skills and interests present in the class. When teachers plan the richer, more challenging learning experiences characteristic of a MAG classroom, all the children enjoy a more equal opportunity to succeed, a necessary ingredient in building self-confidence.

Many Opportunities to Be Leaders and Followers

Within a MAG classroom, as in a family, there are many natural opportunities to assume both the role of follower and leader, and to build a sense of independence and responsibility. **There is no necessity to establish potentially artificial links with other children in other classrooms**, such as Buddy Reading. Children naturally buddy with each other in a variety of ongoing learning situations within the confines of their own secure classroom to learn new concepts and skills. And loners and children who have difficulty in forming relationships enjoy the special benefit of having more time and opportunity to select a comfortable, non-threatening learning partner — they have all day, every day to build this relationship.

We know that children need many opportunities to demonstrate and practise newly acquired knowledge, skills and attitudes. As followers, in learning a new concept or skill, learners have the chance to be part of non-threatening demonstrations by peers. As leaders, learners have many chances to practise and consolidate their understandings. The MAG classroom provides more opportunities for demonstrating and practising than the traditional classroom.

The abilities to lead and to follow are important for learners to develop if they are to play a variety of roles and become successful citizens. Over a two- or three-year period, all children in a MAG classroom have many occasions in which to develop these skills. They can thereby become both leaders and followers in cooperative, collaborative work and leisure groupings.

Increased self-confidence results when all children have invitations to play and experiment with all roles. While such invitations are evident in a MAG classroom, in single-age classrooms, often the same children are always leaders — only a few hold the more developed skills.

More Sources of Help and Guidance

No longer is the teacher the only expert who can read or tie shoes. As in a family setting, many sources of help, support, guidance, and encouragement are available in MAG classrooms. This more efficient structure lets children proceed with their learning without having to wait for the one adult expert. There are many teachers and support systems that learners can access.

Learners have more opportunities to find guidance and help from someone whose learning style might be more compatible with their own. **We have found that children often learn more effectively when they seek help from children who have just recently acquired the skills and understanding of the process.** Sometimes, children feel nervous about asking for help from adults whom they perceive to be experts and able to do everything perfectly. Many adults have long forgotten how they learned, making it difficult for them to help new learners "crack the code." Children often have a more succinct and clear way of helping their peers overcome difficulties in the learning process.

In MAG classes the children themselves add to the support system, providing a unique way of communicating new learning. On the other hand, teachers in single-grade classrooms will sometimes invite adult volunteers to assist when they realize that children require individual help when learning. Unfortunately, the MAG process of learning is often misunderstood by parents and educators. Often, it is viewed as a detriment to the more competent learners and as wasteful of their time.

In reality, encouraging children to help one another is an important ingredient in the learning process: it helps more competent learners to clarify, consolidate, practise and communicate their own understandings. They have an opportunity to refine their own learning in a non-threatening situation. They can feel more confident and competent. They learn to be sensitive to learners of differing abilities. They practise the basic skills of teaching/learning in situations where they learn to observe, to assess and evaluate, and to offer the necessary support and guidance. This development occurs naturally in such a supportive family-like atmosphere.

We believe students are advantaged because of these opportunities. Life today at home, in the community, and in the work place requires that we develop such skills, knowledge and attitudes. Wrote David Pratt in "On the Merits of Multiage Classrooms," "The evidence on Multiage grouping appears to confirm the basic principle that diversity enriches and uniformity impoverishes." [*Research in Rural Education* 3 (3): 111–15]

More Time to Build Positive Relationships

Another major advantage, from our perspective, is that children, parents and teachers all have more time to build and develop more positive long-term relationships. **As in a family, all members have time to feel secure enough to develop trust and risk-taking confidence.** Unlike traditional settings where a ten-month term is available, MAG classes have up to thirty months to establish these important relationships. Children are not uprooted yearly for organizational purposes. We believe that annual class/teacher/classroom change serves only to interrupt this all-important relationship between teachers, parents and children.

Relationships Between Teachers and Children

Teachers and children need more than ten months to learn about each other and to learn about the specific routines and expectations of their work together. It also takes considerable time to establish the necessary comfort level that young children need to fully demonstrate their competencies. For example, one child might need a full year to muster the courage to speak in front of the class during discussions. When uprooted, the child may become silent again, and confidence often wanes. Had the child been able to continue in the same setting with a familiar teacher and peers, confidence could have blossomed.

Relationships Between Children and Children

There is also more time in a MAG classroom for the children to build positive relationships with others of different ages. Even when the teacher is unable to continue for an extended period of time with the class, the children still benefit from belonging to such a secure, trusting peer group. They provide continued support for one another.

This mutual benefit mirrors what happens in many family contexts where children learn to share, respect, trust, help, and compromise and cooperate with siblings, even when the family unit experiences changes; perhaps a death, a divorce, a relocation. These social skills are necessary if one is to become a successful member of the larger community.

Relationships Between Teachers and Parents

As educators we have always valued the importance of a strong partnership between parents/guardians or caregivers and teachers. Research has shown that children benefit when parents and teachers share the responsibility for education. A

Toronto Board of Education document, *Academically Successful Inner City Children: What They Can Tell Us About Effective Education*, 1989, confirms this.

Partnerships take time to develop. The additional time that MAG classrooms provide allows for such partnerships and relationships to develop more fully. Both partners develop a trust and an understanding of each other's role. Together, they explore the ways in which individual children learn best.

It has been our experience that parents have many questions for the teacher about teaching and learning.

> In a Grade 1/2/3 classroom a mother asked the teacher why her child's spelling errors were not all corrected. Because the teacher knew her and understood her perspective, she was able to remind the parent of the progress that had been made since last year, locate where the child was currently on the spelling continuum, and share her plans for future spelling instruction.

This kind of parent education demands extended periods of time. Because we had such a strong relationship with our parents, we were able to build a better understanding of how young children learn. Classroom visits, interviews, and informal discussions were frequent and occurred naturally, relieving many anxieties and concerns about the education of young children. As teachers share their expertise and knowledge, parents become valued advocates.

This type of in-depth relationship is difficult to develop in a traditional setting where time is so short. In many Kindergarten classrooms, teachers are required to develop this all-important relationship with as many as fifty sets of parents. A formidable task! In the context of a year the teacher cannot establish and develop this relationship to its fullest. Yet this time is so important in the educational experience of young children. We believe that these initial impressions and relationships color future attitudes towards school and learning. The findings of a recent Ontario Royal Commission on Learning support this belief.

More Efficient Use of Time

In MAG classrooms teachers need to spend considerably less time acquainting the children with the necessary classroom routines. New children arrive in a school setting where many classmates are already familiar with the classroom routines and operations. These classmates know the "ropes" and can model for newcomers as well as lend a helpful hand where necessary.

> When Una taught a Junior Kindergarten classroom she spent many weeks introducing, demonstrating and reinforcing the painting routine — where to get your paper, what to do if a spill occurs, where to print your name, how to avoid drips, etc. In a JK/SK/Grade 1 setting these tasks were taken over naturally by the children. They became the teachers, demonstrating and supporting the newcomers. There was always a friend available to help a child know what to do next!

With many classroom activities already successfully underway, the new children can pick up the mechanics of how the room operates quite quickly and with better long-term understanding. For example: Upon initial entry the teacher does not have to remind the class of the entrance routine. Experienced members of the class carry out the routine naturally, providing a model for the less experienced children to imitate. In addition, **with two-thirds of the class behaving in an independent manner, the teacher has more time to spend with new, small groups of children, introducing or reinforcing routines.** This "getting acquainted" takes less time and is less stressful since many children already know what to do and can assist. Under such conditions, children enter with less anxiety and usually establish a comfort level more quickly. More time is then afforded for the teacher to teach or work with individuals and small groups.

Multi-age groupings permit a smoother orientation. This orientation occurs only once upon entry into the three-year program. Time is not lost each September in relearning and re-establishing necessary academic, behavioral and social expectations. We believe that young children are disadvantaged when they do not have a full knowledge of the teacher's expectations, limits and routines. In traditional settings it often takes three months or the entire first term to establish first-hand knowledge of what the teacher expects and requires from children. For example: When children finish a painting or a piece of writing, they need to make decisions about the next step in the process. Is it complete? Does it need more work? Where does it need to be filed? Two-thirds of the children in a MAG class can readily answer such questions at the beginning of the first term.

In addition, teachers in MAG classrooms do not need to spend much time each year becoming acquainted with the developmental levels of a whole class of new learners. Since the majority of the children continue to progress from where they left off in June, the teacher can make more efficient use of time to assess new children, modify curriculum plans and get on with the business of teaching. Teachers in these settings have more time to develop an in-depth knowledge of and insight into the strengths and areas for growth of each child.

More Opportunities for Choice of Placement

When the time does come to move one-third of the children to new classrooms, more choices are available in a school that is organized in a MAG manner. Because more options are available, administrators and teachers can make better decisions about the best match for teachers and children in terms of learning styles and personalities. There are more opportunities for children who do not work well together to be separated; for example, in a school where there are two Kindergarten classrooms, two Grade 1 classrooms and two Grade 2 classrooms as separate options for placement, the choice is limited. However, if these six settings became MAG grouped, the options for placement would increase significantly, allowing more appropriate matches to be found for teachers, children and parents.

Easier Transition from Home to School

Transitions at any time in life can cause regression, stress, trauma or any combination of these problems. When young children first come to school, they often find it frightening. Research shows that children who have a positive experience when they enter school tend to meet with more academic success than those who have not. First impressions are crucial.

Teachers in MAG classrooms can spend more time supporting each newcomer and their family through this important experience. That is because they receive only a few new children each year. On the other hand, supporting newcomers is difficult when everyone in the class is new, each simultaneously needing the reassurance of only one teacher at the same time.

Children in a MAG setting enter into an invitational classroom that is well established, happy, and secure. This is in stark contrast to a traditional one-age classroom where everyone is new, some are bewildered and insecure, and all are required, simultaneously, to get used to the new setting. The classrooms are often bare or decorated with commercial posters and pictures. In the MAG classroom, the walls are far from bare. They are covered with work from the previous June.

Many exciting activities are already underway in the MAG classroom. Traditionally, however, teachers provide only a few activities in September and add new learning centres as the children become more familiar with the routines and expectations. MAG teachers can move more quickly since two-thirds of the class already know the routines and expectations. These children provide assistance and help to the newcomers. They help to make this first experience in school less threatening — even adults appreciate a knowledgeable friend or buddy when they are approaching a new task, place or experience.

The smoothly operating MAG classroom looks to newcomers like a terrific place to be. Some have suggested that a room such as we have described may overwhelm newcomers. On the contrary, we find the opposite to be true. Many new children forget their initial reluctance, find a friend and eagerly get started on their educational careers.

Enhanced Learning

Recent research presented by Brian Cambourne in *The Whole Story* (Auckland, N.Z.: Ashton-Scholastic, 1988) suggests that certain conditions support learning.

Just as in a healthy family, children in a MAG classroom find themselves in a relaxed atmosphere that is conducive to promoting these conditions. These important conditions are immersion, expectation, response, demonstration, approximation, responsibility, and practice. When they are present, learners become truly engaged in the learning process!

- **Immersion** in a richer environment exposes children to a wider range of meaningful learning experiences and stimulating materials.
- The **expectation** is that all children will succeed.
- **Feedback/positive responses** encourage children to take risks, and enjoyment and success provide immediate incentives to children to keep striving.
- Varying levels of competence in the room, besides that of the teacher, provide encouraging models of **instruction** and **demonstrations** for the interested young audience.
- Because the children are all at different levels, all **approximations** are encouraged, expected and respected. Children are invited to take risks, to have a go and to move towards increasingly accurate conventions and skills. They are not all expected to do the same thing at the same time. Differences are blurred and do not stand out for critical evaluation or comparison.
- Children are encouraged to take **responsibility** for their own learning by making choices and decisions about their learning and work.
- More chances for **meaningful practice** exist as more sophisticated learners help new learners. We believe that children need to be active, self-directed and responsible for their own learning.

For us, **the structure of a MAG classroom provides an optimum atmosphere, the necessary time, and learning conditions to promote success.** We agree with Cambourne that there are parallels between learning to speak and learning to read and write. Children naturally imitate the talk of parents and siblings. In addition, children in a MAG classroom have more natural opportunities to observe and imitate reading and writing behaviors. If we expect children to be lifelong readers and writers, they need to see their family members and peers willingly, enthusiastically and over time engaged in these activities. Unlike traditional teachers who often try to replicate these critical conditions by arranging a buddy system with another class, MAG teachers don't need to seek opportunities outside of their own classrooms.

Teachers and academic researchers have recorded many advantages of classes organized around MAG beliefs and practices. Parents, too, have identified the advantages from their own individual child's perspective. We have outlined those advantages that seem most consistent with our own experiences. We personally found *no* disadvantages that we were unable to overcome given increased trust, communication, flexibility, and time. Initially, however, we had to spend time helping parents to understand how children learn most effectively and how the MAG organization supports children as learners. We did this by using a variety of strategies, which included inviting parents to observe work in the classroom and providing information sessions in many languages about the developmental nature of learning. Chapter 12 answers some of parents' most common questions.

We are convinced of the benefits of MAG classrooms for children, parents, teachers and administrators. And in our years in education, we have met many teachers who are as excited as we are about teaching in this way. If *you* share our beliefs about how children learn and see how a MAG classroom supports learning, this book will provide you with practical support.

3/The Learning Environment in a MAG Classroom

Determining the Best Structure

We have always begun our teaching by reflecting on the specifics of the learning environment.

The basic belief system of the teacher determines the learning environment. Some teachers do not believe in empowering the children and so they create learning environments that are very teacher-directed. They make all decisions about what and how learning takes place. On the other hand, we want to create an optimum learning environment where children and the teacher share responsibility for directing the learning. Critical components include the learning climate, learning styles, decision-making processes, the timetable, the physical organization, evaluation techniques and varying roles of the participants. We believe in using a variety of instructional techniques, demonstrations, mini-lessons and conferences that suit the developmental needs of students. As a result, we always ask ourselves the following key questions:

- What organizational structure will work best?
- How will the classroom operate?
- How will we timetable to ensure the most efficient use of teacher and student time?
- How do we plan learning centres in order to maximize the learning for all children?

We address the first three questions in this chapter and explore the workings of various learning centres in chapters 4 to 11.

An Organizational Structure That Works: Learning Centres

We found that establishing a non-threatening atmosphere where risk taking was encouraged provided a good place to begin.

The best organizational structure for doing this features permanent and temporary centres, with the classroom arranged specifically to accommodate them. However, it is not enough to merely create centres. Some teachers have difficulty trusting children's choices and so they assign learning tasks or rotate children through a variety of learning experiences. Also, as children grow older, teachers often abandon learning centres in favor of whole-class, lecture-style instructional techniques. Children in the Primary division need hands-on, active learning opportunities just as much as children in Kindergarten classes.

Overemphasis on teacher-directed paper and pencil tasks does not respect children's differing developmental levels. Nor does it allow for the key learning conditions of ownership, relevance, response and varied expectations to occur.

We found that organizing our activities into learning centres was the best way to manage the space available. In most classrooms, space is limited. Every child cannot have their own work space as well as access to learning centres. Desks inhibit collaborative learning and prevent easy access to learning activities. Children need space to be active, to explore, to design, to construct and to learn together.

The following centres are a must in any Kindergarten or Primary classroom: visual arts, writing/drawing, reading, sand table, water table, interest, construction materials, and home.

These centres provide learning opportunities for children to acquire the skills, knowledge and attitudes that educational authorities generally prescribe. The four major subject areas of the curriculum can be integrated into the centres.

This organization allows children to learn in small groups, large groups or individually, at a variety of activities. The selection and involvement are largely self-directed. However, after careful tracking and record keeping, the teacher may limit or extend student choices. The purpose is to better meet children's learning needs, such as introducing a child to paints.

Each classroom presents its own challenges and limitations in terms of space and equipment. As we first set up a physical environment we considered the need for the following:

- easy access to the materials — children should be able, independently, to get them out and put them away
- quiet places for students who need them
- areas for water/sand activities
- space for small-group activities
- a place for everyone to gather
- space for traffic flow

We preferred that the children work at tables rather than individual desks so that we could thereby encourage cooperative and collaborative learning. We grouped the furniture to form centres. We provided the children with their own basins or cubbies for personal treasures. Basic supplies were stored at the appropriate centres and shared by all.

LEARNING CENTRES

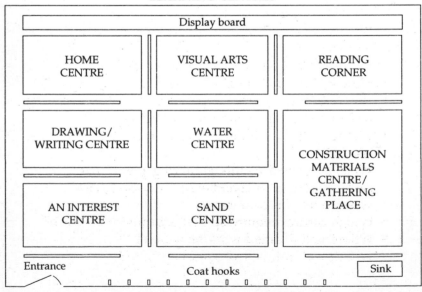

Here is a flexible and efficient layout for a classroom with key learning centres.

Questions About Setting Up Learning Centres

Here is a list of questions that teachers setting up MAG classrooms should consider. There is no right way to answer these questions.

- How will you arrange the furniture (desks or tables) to accommodate the necessary centres?
- How will you accommodate the various physical sizes of the children?
- Where will the children keep their personal belongings? In a box or basket? In a cubby hole?
- Where will storage containers be kept? On shelves? In an open cupboard?
- How will the children know where they should work?
- Can the children move freely in the room?
- Do the children have adequate room to work?
- Is there too much furniture in the room?
- Which centres will be ready for use on the first day? (*Remember*: In MAG classrooms, two-thirds of the class were in the room last year and they are eager to continue their work where they left off.)
- When will you add new centres? Every week? Every two weeks?
- In what order will you add the centres?
- How will the supplies be shared?
- Where will the shared supplies be kept? At each centre? At a separate communal supply centre?
- Where will the students gather for a story or mini-lesson?
- What is needed at this gathering place? A chair? An easel? A carpet? A chalkboard? A pocketchart?
- Where will you conference?
- Which centres require special equipment or space?
- Where will finished work be stored?
- Where will unfinished work be stored?

Efficient Classroom Management

The Importance of Routines

Our experience has been that the centres in our rooms were more successful when routines were explicit and meaningful. To help achieve this, in our MAG classrooms the children had input in creating the routines. For example, they might say, "The water table is too crowded. Maybe two people instead of three should go there." They also helped to monitor the success of the routines and made suggestions for changes where necessary during regularly held classroom discussions. Since the classroom was *for the children*, we believed then and do now that the orchestration of the environment must involve them as much as possible.

Routines must be carefully introduced to the children if they are to succeed. In a single-grade/age classroom this process is often frustrating and usually takes a very long time. **However, in our MAG classrooms, many children were familiar with the routines and eager to take on leadership roles and responsibilities for the introduction and reinforcement of routines.** Centres were therefore established more meaningfully and quickly.

Our goal was for children to use the centres independently, assuming responsibility for many of the housekeeping chores in the busy MAG classroom. We, as teachers, were then able to concentrate on the more important tasks, instructing, coaching, facilitating, listening, questioning, and supporting.

Effective Timetables

As experienced teachers who had honed their understanding of a centred approach to learning, we preferred to have all of the centres open during each work period.

Many teachers, however, struggle with this time frame. With such a wide selection of activities and developmental levels, they report that they are unable to spend as much time as they

Some Questions to Consider When Developing Routines

Here are some key ones:
- How many children can work safely at each centre?
- How will the children know how many can work at each centre?
- What supplies will be needed?
- Where will the supplies be stored?
- Who will be responsible for replenishing the supplies?
- What materials will be needed for an efficient and effective tidy up?
- Who will be responsible for the tidy up?
- How will the children know who is responsible?
- How will the children know to stop and listen?

need interacting with the children and supporting their learning. They are equally uncomfortable with the old work and play periods in which children complete teacher-directed tasks first, and then are allowed, time permitting, to select activities from their own interests.

Achieving a Manageable Focus

Recently, some teachers in MAG classrooms structured their day so that there are two distinct activity periods. One period focuses on literacy and the arts. It features such learning centres as the reading corner, home centre, writing/drawing centre, visual arts centre and interest centre. The other activity period focuses on activities with a math/science/technology focus, opening up the big blocks, construction materials, sand and water centres. Teachers report that they can focus better with such a timetable.

Teachers can plan a more manageable focus. For example, early in the year at the writing centre, a teacher might want to teach the children how to print their own names. Teachers feel they have the time necessary to introduce, support and reinforce this critical routine as well as teach the children the skill when only half of the learning centres are open. They also report that they can plan to spend more time at each of the centres observing, modelling and extending the learning. In rooms where all of the activities were open at the same time, the teachers found it hard to spend quality time at each centre.

Often teachers new to MAG classrooms overlook the math/science/technology activities, such as big blocks, in favor of working at reading and writing centres. With the split-focus organization, time is spent equally in all areas. Just as time is spent helping children write their own stories, it is also spent helping children to pour and measure with increasing accuracy. In such an organization the teacher's behavior makes it explicit that all of these learning centres are valued equally. In addition, teachers report that children spend quality time in all areas of the curriculum; before, ensuring that children had experiences from all of the important curricula areas was more difficult.

Other important learning experiences, such as physical education, music, stories, snack, and outdoor play, must also be considered when finalizing a timetable. We found that these experiences were inserted easily between the large blocks of time allocated for literacy/arts or math/science/technology. A few examples of timetables that work appear to the right.

The Basis of Success

In summary, successful MAG classrooms rely on careful consideration being given to classroom organization, routines and timetables. They also call for teachers to spend time thinking about why they have these centres, what learning they expect to occur, what materials will support this learning, and what routines are particularly necessary to ensure that children can use the centres independently.

The next eight chapters discuss major centres. They offer a rationale for each of them, lists of materials that encourage learning, questions reflective practitioners might ask themselves, and developmental mileposts to help guide observations of children's interactions with materials and classmates.

Timetable: JK/K/Gr. 1

8:45–9:00	*Entrance; Borrow-a-Book Exchange*
9:00–9:15	*Story — shared reading/writing*
9:15–10:15	*Activity Period — literacy/art; math/science/tech*
10:15–10:30	*Sharing Time*
10:30–10:45	*Recess for Gr. 1s; Snack, Book Time for JK/K*
10:45–11:15	*Music/Drama/Story*
11:15–11:45	*Outdoor Play or Gym for JK/K; Gr. 1s' Private Reading Time*
11:45	*Dismissal — Gr. 1s begin to tidy up at 11:30*
Lunch	
12:45–1:00	*Entrance; Borrow-a-Book Exchange*
1:00–1:15	*Story — shared reading/writing*
1:15–2:15	*Activity Period — all centres open*
2:15–2:30	*Sharing*
2:30–2:45	*Recess for Gr. 1s; Snack, Book Time for JK/K*
2:45–3:00	*Music/Drama/Story*
3:00–3:45	*Gym for whole class or outdoor play for JK/K and work completion for Gr. 1s*
3:45	*Dismissal*

Timetable: Gr. 1/2/3

8:45–9:00	*Entrance, Book Exchange*
9:00–9.15	*Story — shared reading/writing*
9:15–10:15	*Literacy/Art Work Period*
10:15–10:30	*Sharing Time*
10:30–10:45	*Recess*
10:45–11:00	*Private Reading Time or Music*
11:00–11:30	*Literacy/Art Work Period or Gym*
11:30–11:45	*Tidy Up; Dismissal*
Lunch	
12:45–1:00	*Entrance, Book Exchange*
1:00–1:15	*Story — shared reading/writing — math focus*
1:15–2:30	*Math/Science/Technology Work Period*
2:30–2:45	*Recess*
2:45–3:15	*Math/Science/Technology Deconstruction/Recording Time*
3:15–3:30	*Sharing Time*
3:30–3:45	*Tidy Up; Dismissal*

4/The Visual Arts Centre

Why a Visual Arts Centre Is Needed in a MAG Classroom

This centre provides the materials that the children use to communicate their ideas and feelings through visual arts. Children often use it to make the props they need for their dramatic play and to demonstrate their understanding and feelings about their many interests.

The visual arts centre is never static, demanding a regular infusion of new materials and techniques. It can become very messy; therefore, routines and organization are very important. For us it has three distinct components: paints, glue and found materials, and modelling materials. We prefer to put all of these areas together. Doing this encourages the children to mix and build on the visual art media, using the materials in more interesting, creative and unique ways.

In single-age classrooms some teachers are tempted to provide precut patterns, stencils or teacher-directed crafts for the children to use at this centre. They may find it particularly tempting to do this around holidays or celebrations such as Mother's Day. We would suggest that teachers always consider the appropriateness of such gifts. If the gift giving seems appropriate, then the children should select what the gift might be, perhaps a card, a drawing, a poem, a photograph, a recording. Some teachers feel that all the children should participate or offer the same gift, and they offer several reasons for these widespread beliefs and practices.

Some teachers believe that, since the children are all of the same age, they should be able to produce the same recognizable product. Others believe the children can't think of ways to create recognizable products and need their patterns, directions, and thinking in order to do so. Still others argue that the children like to be given a model to copy. A majority of teachers tell us that they follow these practices because the parents expect and like them.

We believe that these practices are destructive. They serve only to frustrate children, limit their creativity and erode their confidence as learners. Teacher-imposed activities often result in children saying, "I can't do it," "I'm no good at art," or "Teacher, can you draw a castle for me?" Despite their similar chronological age, the children are at many different places on the learning continuum. Those who are at the manipulative stage of drawing are frustrated because they can't produce a model, for example, a caterpillar out of an egg carton; as yet, they cannot identify or envision the relationship between the concrete object and the abstract symbol. Other children are well able to see this relationship and have much more inventive ways of implementing their ideas than following the teacher's cute model, for example, a candle holder out of a toilet paper roll and paper plate.

When planning activities we always ask ourselves the question "Who is actively engaged in the thinking, problem solving, doing and learning? Teachers or children?" Teacher-prepared work sets many children up to fail and denies all the opportunity to learn through exploration, experience and meaningful instruction. Teachers need to be clear about the outcomes they wish to achieve with children. Do they want them to be copiers or creative problem solvers? followers or leaders? What is the role of the teacher? To limit thinking or extend it? These vital questions permeate the expectations in all areas of the classroom. If we "do" for children in one area of the curriculum such as visual arts, the children will expect us to "do" for them in all areas. We will create children who will not risk or explore the limits of their own potential and who will have a low image of themselves as learners.

In our experience, the only children who have shown any enjoyment in copying the teacher's work are those who wish to please or are often afraid to risk and think for themselves. When asked, children are well aware of who did the work and the thinking. They feel uncomfortable taking credit for the work and often say, "My teacher helped me with these parts." For many others, it is a time of tears, refusal to try, minimal effort, and anger. As Brian Cambourne suggests, when learners see no relevance in or ownership of activities, they disengage and save their energy for more relevant learning.

Parents need to understand that their children are still learning despite the absence of perfectly finished crafts and products. Teachers can inform, educate and reassure them about this. Teachers and parents have important, but different roles to play in the learning. Rather than providing set patterns to copy, adults need to help children to take risks and develop their own ways to represent the world. Parents and teachers need to respond positively to all their children's best efforts. We do not suggest that low standards be accepted, only that the expectations fit the children's individual abilities.

Representing Children's Varied Thinking, Competencies and Interests

In MAG classrooms where the children have such a wide range of developmental levels and abilities, it is counter-productive to expect the children to merely copy the teachers' ideas. Rather, it is expected that the children's creations will represent their varied thinking, competencies and interests. Our role is much more than searching through the latest craft magazines for cute art ideas. When we observe the need and interest of the children, we offer a wide variety of demonstrations of techniques; for example, scoring and curling paper, mixing colors, using different paints/dyes that support their work and help them solve the problems they encounter. **By expecting different results, we set the stage for children to take risks and think creatively.**

The goals we set always help the children extend, consolidate and apply their learning. We focus on the process, not the finished product. All work is valued and expected to be individualized and different. Giving children a precut pattern, such as a gingerbread man that the children are required only to decorate, denies them the opportunity to create their own shape. In the MAG classroom, they are certain to have it.

Children in a MAG classroom are expected to sympathize with and support those who are still at the manipulative stage. We frequently overheard more competent children reassuring others by saying, "I used to draw like that, then I did it this way, and that's what you'll be doing as you get older." Children thrive in such a positive atmosphere.

Materials That Encourage Painting in a MAG Classroom

There is a wider variety of tools and media for painting in a MAG classroom than a traditional classroom. The following are helpful:

- paints of different colors — pastel and primary, and provision for mixing in palettes or muffin tins
- paints of different consistency — thick for blobbing, thin for washes
- brushes of various sizes
- aprons or old shirts, but not plastic garbage bags
- easels and a large table covered with oilcloth or a roll of oilcloth to be used on the floor
- sponges and soapy water for clean-up (Adding a little liquid soap to the paints helps with the clean-up.)

The paint supplies provide their own unique challenge for busy teachers since the quality of the work is directly related to the quality of the materials. Brushes, paints, and paper must be of the highest quality, and paints changed regularly. We kept this centre alive and interesting by introducing new paint techniques in addition to the staple paint and paper supplies. At intervals we added string, straws, sponges, soap flakes, starch, found materials for print making, and finger paint in order to provide a wealth of paint experiences. All the children used the materials in their own creative ways as opposed to everyone making the same snowman pictures with soap flake paint.

Materials That Encourage "Make It" Activities in a MAG Classroom

Materials represent a wider variety than what would be offered in a traditional classroom. The range reflects differing expectations of children's abilities. Plan to offer the following items:

- glue in small plastic containers with their own lids (It's easy to peel dried glue off the sides of these containers or discard them.)
- other glue materials — glue sticks, different kinds of tape
- various weights and sizes of paper kept in cut down cereal boxes or baskets, one box for each color
- scissors — both left- and right-handed
- a collection of everchanging "found" materials — sequins, toothpicks, feathers, pipe cleaners, fabric, small boxes, cardboard rolls, cotton balls, and wool of all colors and weights

All these materials are stored in labelled buckets for easy access and clean-up. We put out only small quantities of available materials to make tidy up more manageable. We also changed the materials in this centre frequently.

In addition, we encouraged the children to bring found materials from their homes to support their interests. At discussion times we explored with them how they might use these materials; for example, a button might be an eye for an animal or its body, or the centre of a flower. Children could practise thinking creatively.

We also gradually introduced new "make it" techniques, such as for one-, two- and three-dimensional work. We provided experiences with paper mâché, crushing, scoring, folding, fringing, pleating, and curling when it was relevant and purposeful for individuals and small groups of interested children. We also continually encouraged the children to use these techniques in future work by asking them how they planned to make their giraffe or snowman. "Will it be flat, two- or three-dimensional? What materials will you need for paper mâché, boxes, fabric, paper? How can you add special features? texture? and so on. Children enjoyed creative ownership of their work.

Materials That Encourage Modelling Activities in a MAG Classroom

Students may enjoy working with these materials:

- cooked playdough
- flour and salt
- play clay
- goop
- plasticene
- clay

These materials were not all available at the same time. Once the children were familiar with the materials and the special techniques of their use, we encouraged them to request them for particular projects throughout the year. These materials need to be stored carefully as they dry out easily. We used airtight containers and freshened and changed the materials regularly. We preferred to make any of the homemade materials with the children so they could observe and experience changes in properties.

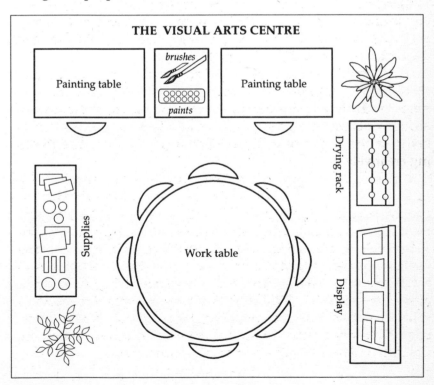

Cooked Playdough

Ingredients

1 c salt
2 c flour
4 tsp cream of tartar
2 tbsp cooking oil
2 cups water
food coloring

Method

- Mix all ingredients in a saucepan.
- Add food coloring.
- Cook on a medium heat for 3-5 minutes. (An adult should do this.)
- Stir constantly until the mixture becomes stiff.
- Store in airtight containers.

Play Clay

Ingredients

1 c corn starch
2 c baking soda
1½ c cold water

Method

- Mix corn starch and baking soda together.
- Add water.
- Cook over a medium heat.
- Stir constantly until the mixture looks like moist mashed potatoes.
- Pour mixture onto a plate and cover with a damp cloth.
- When it cools, knead it like dough.
- Use only a little clay at a time, storing the rest in an airtight container.
- To prevent sticking, work on wax paper or dust the utensils with cornstarch.

Flour and Salt

Ingredients

2 c flour
1 c salt
1 tbsp cooking oil
1 cup water
food coloring

Method

- Mix food coloring with oil and water.
- Add to the dry ingredients.
- Store dough in plastic containers or bags.
- If the dough becomes sticky, add some flour.

Goop

Ingredients

1½ tsp borax powder
8 oz white glue
2 c water
food coloring

Method

- Combine glue, one cup of water and food coloring.
- Dissolve borax in 1 cup of water. (Make sure the borax is completely dissolved.
- Pour first mixture into the borax mixture.
- Mix and knead into a ball!

The Visual Arts Centre in a MAG Classroom: Some
Questions for the Reflective Practitioner to Ask if an
Environment for Success Is to Be Created

1. How do I ensure that the materials are accessible and available on a regular basis, not just at particular times for the children to use?
   • You could schedule daily blocks of time for visual arts each day.
   • You could also encourage the children to use visual arts materials to respond to other areas of the curriculum, such as a story, a trip, an experience from home.

2. How do I ensure that I have samples of work that demonstrate the progress of the children over time?
   • Have the children date all work samples.
   • Provide ongoing work folders for all children.
   • Keep portfolios of selected samples of work for all children.

3. How can I help parents understand the importance of their responses?
   • Send home regular newsletters with suggestions of positive, constructive responses parents can offer their children.
   • Post signs at the centre, highlighting its importance.
   • Regularly use samples of work to discuss the learning that is taking place.

4. How can I help parents to demonstrate that they value child-initiated and completed work rather than adult-imposed and -directed work?
   • Regularly model such behavior by displaying all children's work not just the best or most recognizable.
   • Resist the temptation to impose the same product for all children.
   • Ask yourself what you hope the children will learn from the experience.

5. How do I help all children realize that their work is valued and worthwhile?
   - Be sure to respond positively to the efforts of all the children.
   - Take time to help all the children extend their work.
   - Send work home that elicits parental comments; for example, you could provide a comment page for responses to collaborative books.

6. How do I ensure that I have time to help children extend their learning, consolidate skills, and develop their understanding, skills and attitudes?
   - You could share the responsibility for the maintenance of the room with the more mature children so you have more time to teach.
   - You could encourage the children to check in with you when they have completed their work so you can comment or offer a challenge.
   - You could encourage the children to go to each other or to more sophisticated learners for help and solutions.
   - You could model by asking, "How do you think you might find out the answer to your question?"

7. How do I ensure that the children feel ownership of and responsibility for their work?
   - Have the children select their own topics for inquiry.
   - Encourage the children to make their own decisions about what method they will use.
   - Also, encourage the children to use the centre to respond to other areas of the curriculum, for example, science, language.
   - Invite the children to evaluate their own work and the work of others.

Some Mileposts to Help Guide Teacher Observations of Children Working in the Visual Arts Centre in a MAG Classroom

AT THE PAINTING CENTRE

The Way That Children Use the Brush

They might:

__ use their whole fist

__ use their thumb and fingers

__ hold the end/middle of the brush

__ move between the pot of paint and paper in one movement with no wipes and many drips

__ wipe the excess paint off the brush

The Way That Children Use the Paint

They might:

__ dab paint on the paper using one color

__ scrub the brush over one area with one color

__ experiment with several colors

__ join dabs into curved and straight lines using one or several colors

__ make curved lines into circles and ovals, sometimes filling them in

__ take circles and ovals and lines and begin to make symbols, such as the sun, letters, and numerals

__ take circles and lines and begin to make symbols of body images

__ add more lines, dots and dabs to make a more detailed person, for example, fingers, feet, clothes, hair

__ show houses or apartments that enclose people

__ add recognizable symbols of other familiar objects in the environment such as trees and flowers

__ use other media and found materials, perhaps working with glitter and construction paper

__ adopt a base line and a sky line

__ show profiles, perspective and relative size

AT THE "MAKE IT" CENTRE

The Way That Children Control the Materials

They might:

__ apply glue with fingers, glue brushes or sticks

__ use alternative methods to attach materials, such as tape, stapler, glue sticks

__ use an appropriate amount of glue with control

__ tear materials

__ cut materials with an adult holding the material

__ cut independently with some control

__ cut with increasing control

The Way That Children Use the Found Materials

They might:

__ glue found materials together randomly

__ choose materials randomly

__ make patterns or designs

__ select materials with a specific purpose for 2D and 3D creations

__ work on projects over time until completed

MODELLING MATERIALS

The Way That Children Use the Materials

They might:

__ use hands and fingers to manipulate the materials

__ use other tools, such as blunt plastic cutlery, to manipulate the materials

__ flatten the material using hands or tools

__ experiment with different textures, perhaps scratching or print making

__ roll the material into long rolls or balls

__ add the balls and rolls together to create a 2D or 3D symbol such as a sun, a snowman

__ use other materials to create details

__ use additional modelling material to add details

__ create sculptures by using hands and tools to carve the material

The Way That Children Show Interest in Visual Arts

They might:

__ choose to use art materials to express their ideas, e.g., their response to a story

__ use all of the materials available — paints, modelling materials, found materials

__ use the materials with confidence or need support, encouragement, or reminders

__ try different techniques that are introduced, e.g., sponge painting

__ persevere and complete tasks

__ experiment with new ideas or repeat familiar techniques and compositions

Be sure to remember the developmental nature of children's learning when making observations. Skills, knowledge, and interests are not acquired in a lockstep, linear, sequential manner. Children move back and forth on the continuum according to their experiences, circumstances and materials. These mileposts, and others listed in the following chapters, are offered merely as a guide and are not intended to be prescriptive or rigid. It is not expected that all children will demonstrate all of these learnings in the order they are presented. Teachers who listen to and watch their children closely will undoubtedly observe other behaviors and learning.

5/The Reading Corner

If we want children to value reading and to enjoy reading, we, as teachers, must show our enthusiasm and excitement about books and other reading materials.

We did this in our MAG classrooms by creating a large space in a corner that provided a wide range of reading materials and comfortable opportunities for their use. The reading materials appealed to children of different ages, abilities and interests. We learned that it was essential to design such a corner which celebrates books and reading materials, builds excitement and is conducive to the creation of those conditions which support the development of literacy. The mere presence of books throughout the room does not invite children into print.

Fostering Language Learning Effectively

In this corner dedicated to reading, children were immersed in a rich selection of reading materials. The corner allowed the children to select materials that interested them and suited their level of reading ability. It needed to be comfortable and secure and to have an atmosphere and organization that invited children to participate in the process of reading. Children readily took ownership of their own choices.

The nonjudgmental atmosphere and safe space permitted children to grow well as readers. Teachers and other readers provided regular meaningful demonstrations, offered positive feedback and provided relevant opportunities for beginning readers to practise. In a MAG classroom, there are many more sophisticated language users, besides the teacher, to do this. **As the children interact with the teacher and their classmates, they naturally begin to imitate the reading behaviors of successful readers.** Similarly, there are many more coaches to help struggling readers overcome stumbling blocks. Older children have extra opportunities to clarify and practise their new language, knowledge and skills.

Promoting a Love of Reading

For children to develop positive attitudes about reading and to read for a variety of purposes, we needed to select the materials with care. It was essential to include a wealth of reading materials of the highest quality; for example, award-winning authors and illustrators. If all the children were to find materials that were relevant to them, we needed to ensure that these materials were bias free and representative of many different races, cultures and linguistic groups.

We wanted to keep this centre inviting, so we regularly added books borrowed from the library or other teachers. We also heightened the children's awareness of and interest in the works of different authors and illustrators by creating a Favorite Authors Table. It was a dynamic corner.

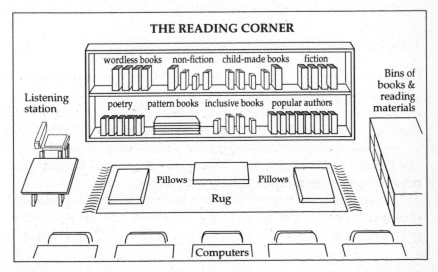

THE READING CORNER

wordless books   non-fiction   child-made books   fiction

Bins of books & reading materials

Listening station

poetry   pattern books   inclusive books   popular authors

Pillows   Pillows

Rug

Computers

Some teachers like to color-code books according to levels of reading difficulty. Children can still make selections from the entire collection, however. The intention of the color coding is not to limit the children's selections, but rather, to help the teacher and children make successful selections for independent reading.

Other teachers showcase the books that have been read aloud to the class by adding multiple copies of paperback versions to the borrow-a-book program.

All of these practices help children love books and spend many happy hours choosing to read.

Materials That Encourage Children in a MAG Classroom to Use the Reading Corner to Read

Here is a workable outline of the physical setup of a reading corner.

- Ideally you would have a good size space complete with a rocking chair, carpet, cuddly toys, listening station and cushions to encourage the children to browse, listen to stories read aloud, read to each other and imitate successful readers.
- Provide a wide variety of bias-free books in good condition that represent many different genres, forms, cultures, races and linguistic groups.
- You could use a movable, open, book-shelving unit that allows you to display books attractively with the covers of many showing.
- Book collections should be frequently changed by the teacher.
- Provide a station where children can listen to audiotapes while following the books.
- Easily available writing materials will allow children to write notes about the books they like or dislike. These reviews can be posted on a board in the reading corner.

The Reading Corner in a MAG Classroom: Some Questions for the Reflective Practitioner to Ask if an Environment for Success Is to Be Created

1. How do I ensure that the centre remains inviting and bias free?
   - Change the books regularly, culling books which are worn, biased and no longer of interest to the children.
   - Borrow new books from the library or from a neighbor.
   - Purposefully select books to support children's interests and to reflect different cultures, gender roles, languages.
   - Highlight favorite and award-winning authors and illustrators.
   - Add multiple copies of favorite read-aloud texts or books.

2. How do I ensure that the books are efficiently organized so children and adults can easily find the materials they want?
   - You could arrange the books according to interest or topic.
   - Consider color-coding the books according to levels of reading difficulty.
   - Display the books so covers are visible.
   - Appoint children as monitors to help younger children browse and make selections.

3. How do I ensure that the children use this corner regularly?
   - Timetable yourself each day to spend time there reading and talking with children about their selections.
   - Provide large blocks of time for reading activities.
   - Make this centre one of the choices available to the children during the activity period. This centre is an integral part of the literacy program, not something just to be enjoyed when "real" work is completed.

4. How do I ensure that I have time to read with the children?
   - Set aside a time each day to read with them. *Prioritize* but be realistic, for example, schedule four children a day.
   - Schedule time for children to read to each other. Doing this is easier in a MAG classroom due to the presence of a wide range of more competent readers.

Some Mileposts to Help Guide Teacher Observations of Children Reading in a MAG Classroom

The Ways That Children Show Interest in Books
They might:
___ voluntarily look at books
___ take on the role of a reader with other children and favorite toys
___ ask for favorite stories to be read
___ point at the illustrations and labels
___ point at the pictures and make up their own stories
___ notice when parts are changed or left out
___ repeat stories from memory
___ borrow books to share with family members
___ select the reading corner as an activity during the literacy time
___ talk about book preferences, authors and illustrators
___ link books together — commenting on similar subject matter, authors or illustrators

The Knowledge That Children Have About Books
They might know the following:
___ how to hold the books the right side up
___ how to turn the pages carefully from front to back of the book
___ that print in English goes from left to right, top to bottom
___ that print and pictures are different
___ what some standard features of the text are: the title, author's name, illustrator's name, dedication
___ that print holds meaning
___ that the pictures help tell the story
___ that sounds and letters have a relationship
___ that there are different kinds of print

The Skills and Strategies That Children Use

They might:
__ read their own name in a different context
__ read the names of others such as siblings and peers
__ recognize environmental print
__ memorize simple familiar texts which have a strong pattern and a good relationship between the pictures and the text
__ skip words they don't know
__ use the pictures as clues to read new text
__ use the structure of the sentences to read unfamiliar text
__ use knowledge of the sound of letters to check approximations for new words
__ reread parts of the text when the meaning is lost
__ when reading non-fiction material, use the title, sub-headings, table of contents to find specific information
__ use different reading strategies to read different genres; for example, in reading expository text, we begin and end reading in varying places and read in chunks.

These developmental mileposts are guidelines only and are not intended to be all-inclusive or prescriptive.

6/The Drawing/Writing Centre

Why a Drawing/Writing Centre Is Needed in a MAG Classroom

The drawing/writing centre is the primary centre where children are invited to draw and write on a frequent basis. However, it is by no means the only place where children write or draw. Writing materials can be found at many of the other centres in the room.

Unlike many of our colleagues, we preferred, in our MAG classrooms, to have a centre rather than an assigned time where everyone was expected and perhaps pressured to write. When given choice, we observed that even children at the scribble stage showed interest in and gravitated towards this centre. The example of the more sophisticated writers naturally motivated them.

Writing seemed to flourish in this atmosphere where children were expected, but not pressured to write in some form or another. At this centre many informal demonstrations took place, and the more sophisticated writers willingly and naturally answered the queries of the beginning writers. They supported each others' efforts to write in the same way that other skills and learning are supported in the family.

We found that writing flourished and children saw themselves as writers naturally in our MAG classrooms. The more competent children helped to introduce, support and reinforce the writing routines. We had many opportunities to conference with the children about their writing and to offer specific instruction or mini-lessons to both individuals and to small groups of children.

We had time to help students with specific skills, including phonics, spelling, punctuation and grammar; with revision; and with the editing process. We had many opportunities to respond to their writing and to offer feedback and suggestions for future work.

Our writing centres ran smoothly for many reasons. The routines were well established. We ensured that the children had real purposes for writing, introducing them to various formats, including letters, lists, records, recipes, directions, signs, stories, poetry. We scheduled time each day for a set number of children to read and share their work with the teacher, both in rough and final draft. Other children had opportunities to provide feedback, suggestions and encouragement about the pieces of work shared. All pieces of writing were accepted and valued. The children themselves saw the positive changes in their own work as well as that of their classmates.

The children became knowledgeable about the wide range of competency on the writing continuum. They were often heard to say, "I used to use all capitals like you do. Soon, you'll be using small letters and capitals just like me." Hearing this reassured the beginning writers about their own efforts. It also reinforced their understanding about the continuous nature of learning. **In being able to point out progress to other children, the more sophisticated writers gained additional practice, confidence and pride in their own writing skills.** They saw the progress they had made.

Our experience with young writers taught us the importance of children selecting their own topics. This ownership of writing fostered the children's interest in and true engagement with the learning. We assured all our children, including the beginners, that they had many interests to write about, stories to tell and purposes for doing so. We encouraged the children to keep, in their writing folders, a list of prospective interests or topics for future writing. In this way we never had any of them say, "I don't know what to write about." We found that if we provided topics and unfamiliar story starters the children were less motivated; they were prevented from writing for authentic reasons. Rather than imposing topics, we spent our time teaching the children the techniques and skills they needed for their writing; for example, dialogue, narrative form, interviews, reports, questions.

We recognized that many children use conventional print, make marks and create pictures before they come to school. Regardless of economic and social background, almost all children have had some exposure to print. Even if their parents were illiterate, the world around them (banks, social assistance offices, television) would have provided models of writing.

We believe that very young children can write and have many stories to tell. Therefore, we provided invitations to write from the very first day at school. **In a MAG classroom the new children have many models of successful writers.**

Developing Writing Skills Early

In the past we used to write for the children, accepting their dictations and believing that they were too young to write for themselves — we even wrote the children's names for them. After dictating their ideas, the children often copied our work, inserting a few words they had memorized. However, as we reflected on this practice, we came to realize that the children were not participating in the real process of writing. We were doing all the thinking and problem solving. As a result, even at the beginning of the year with the very youngest of the children, we asked them to write.

Now we help the children to write their names for themselves. We provide name cards in both capital and small letters for the children to use as a reference. We accept their approximations of these names; for example, some children could represent their name only with a mark, others could copy some of the letters, and still others could write their whole name independently. See the four representative samples above.

We expect a wide range of performances dependent upon their previous writing experiences: scribble, letter attempts, single letters, clusters of letters, recognizable words.

The children made progress in their writing when we provided both formal and informal conferences. At the beginning, we helped the children with the formation of the letters, the sound symbol relationships and the context in which the word they were working with appeared in the whole sentence. As for more mature writers, we met with individuals and groups to focus on particular skills. The children kept a record in their writing folders of the specific grammar, punctuation and spelling rules on which they were working. We also helped the children with other aspects of writing, such as story structure, content and format.

In addition, we encouraged the children to use the computers to communicate. We found that they came to school with varying degrees of experience with computers. Some were very computer literate, knowing how to operate the machine, while others had only seen them on a store shelf or in a newspaper flyer. We resisted the temptation to use the computer only for games, preferring to let the children use it as a tool for a multitude of communication purposes. They used the computer, as they would a pencil, to compose, edit and publish their work. The children were encouraged to use both pencils and computers to communicate.

In MAG classrooms, with the range of ages and competencies, many computer tutors were readily available. The more proficient computer users helped the beginners to become more competent. We usually scheduled two children at a time at a computer so they could support each other. Grouping the children in this way ensured that the use of the computer was socially interactive instead of isolating. The computers were used throughout the day. When there was a demand for additional time to compose, edit or publish, we made arrangements with the librarian to use the library computers. Parent volunteers and co-op students helped the children learn to type and edit using a computer.

Materials That Encourage Children in a MAG Classroom to Write and Draw

The following supplies are helpful:

- paper of many sizes, shapes and weights
- pencils of many thicknesses and colors
- markers of varying thicknesses and colors
- a computer and access to as many computers as possible
- rulers, date stamps
- motivational materials, such as post-it notes, tags, envelopes, notepads, blank labels, cards
- scissors, glue sticks, tape, staplers, paper clips
- other materials specific to writing, including alphabet boards, strips and books, and picture and bilingual dictionaries
- two personal writing folders for each child, one for finished work and one for work in progress
- hanging file folders to hold work-in-progress folders

The Drawing/Writing Centre in a MAG Classroom: Some Questions for the Reflective Practitioner to Ask if an Environment for Success Is to Be Created

1. How do I efficiently and accurately track the children's progress?
   - You could provide each child with one file folder for work in progress.
   - Store this work in easily accessible, hanging file folders.
   - Store all other work in file folders that can be kept in your filing cabinet.
   - Avoid an overload of paper by regularly culling finished work, keeping some for reporting purposes and sending the rest home.
   - Ask the children to date-stamp all work.
   - Ensure that the children save all drafts and samples of brainstorming for future reference.
   - Have children who feel comfortable with the writing process record the titles of their writings and their future plans.
   - Briefly record, in their writing folders, the results of all conversations about particular skills or knowledge. For example, you might note the first time a child uses capital letters or makes the beginning of a story more interesting.
   - You could use the inside of the folders for all notations about ongoing work.

2. How do I ensure that I have samples of the children's work easily available for reporting to parents at parent/teacher conferences?
   - You could have the children date-stamp all work.
   - Keep all work until appropriate selections can be made for sharing with parents. Sharing work every month avoids "paper buildup."
   - Teach the children to make selections from their finished work files that *they* want to share with their parents. In MAG classrooms the older children can greatly help younger children make these choices.

- Schedule time, each month, for you to select pieces of work that you feel show progress, to share with parents.
- Encourage parents and other caregivers to contribute special pieces of work that the children have done at home.
- Keep these significant pieces of work in the students' individual portfolios.
- Give these cumulative portfolios to the teachers the students have next year.

3. How do I ensure that all the children are challenged but not pressured?
   - You could expose the children to a rich variety of authors and their writing styles.
   - Introduce the children to interesting techniques of print and illustrations. For example: The letter format in the Ahlbergs' *Jolly Postman*.
   - Schedule regular times for authentic small-group, shared writing experiences such as writing thank-you notes, invitations, and newsletters for parents.
   - Pair more sophisticated writers with beginning writers.
   - Pair strong writers with strong illustrators sometimes.
   - Provide some writing tasks that require the children to retell, report, rewrite, continue, predict endings and reflect on their work.
   - Schedule time for the children to share their work informally with their peers and formally with a larger group, perhaps another class, other staff members or parents.
   - Focus on what children can do, what they have learned and what they need to learn next in order to create an atmosphere where children are ready to risk.
   - Treat all mistakes as valid attempts and as opportunities to learn.
   - Focus on only a few teaching points at a time so as not to overwhelm and discourage the children.
   - Spend equal time with all the children so that they can see that you value all the learning, whether it be first-time scribbles or conventional print.
   - Schedule a manageable number of children to interact with each day.

4. How can I help parents support their children's efforts to write?
   - Share children's progress regularly, highlighting mileposts.
   - Share with parents the consequences of overcorrecting spelling attempts. Overcorrection erodes self-confidence and the willingness to take risks; it often inhibits the children's writing.
   - Share with parents the specific ongoing spelling instruction you have planned and implemented.
   - Hold a series of discussions throughout the year to respond to writing issues.
   - Encourage the parents of the older children to reassure other parents and to share their children's experiences and successes.

5. How do I incorporate the teaching of spelling, grammar and punctuation rules into the writing program?
   - You could use some of each child's own writing to develop a personal list of frequently misspelled words to be stored in the child's writing folder.
   - Update this spelling list frequently, removing learned words and adding new ones as necessary — keep the list short and current.
   - Have the children use their personal spelling lists to check their work for spelling errors before bringing writing for further editing.
   - Hold daily mini-lessons with the whole class or small groups on observed common errors.

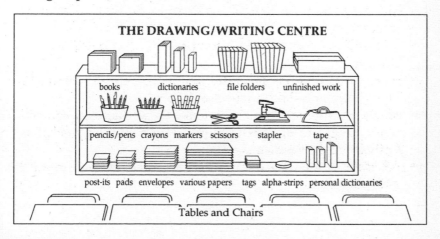

THE DRAWING/WRITING CENTRE

books   dictionaries   file folders   unfinished work

pencils/pens crayons markers scissors   stapler   tape

post-its pads envelopes various papers   tags alpha-strips personal dictionaries

Tables and Chairs

Some Mileposts to Help Guide Teacher Observations of Children's Writing and Drawing in a MAG Classroom

The Way That Children Use Writing/Drawing Tools

They might hold the pencil, marker, crayon, chalk as follows:

___ with the whole fist
___ with their thumb and fingers
___ at the end, middle, or point
___ with increasing control — placing the marks in the intended spot

For the purposes of observation, we have divided the mileposts into two separate continua: drawing and writing. However, in the beginning stages, children do not differentiate between these two processes. They naturally make marks to communicate their ideas and, as they make a mark on a paper for the first time, they intuitively see themselves as writers. However, as they gain more control of their small muscles, develop their eye/hand coordination skills, gain experience with the media and print in their environment, see others writing, and are invited to write themselves, they begin to separate the drawing and writing processes. To continue to see themselves as writers, they must be invited to write and expected to write, they must see other people write, and they must have their efforts accepted and valued.

The Way That Children Use the Drawing Materials for Drawing

They might:

___ experiment with one color or two, making marks that may hold changing meaning for them, but are unrecognizable to adults
___ use or experiment with more than one color
___ use more than one tool
___ join the marks into curved and straight lines using one or several colors

_ make curved lines into circles and ovals, sometimes filling the shapes in

_ take circles and ovals and lines and begin to make symbols, e.g., the sun, letters, numerals

_ take circles and lines and begin to make symbols of body images

_ add more lines and dots to make a more detailed person, e.g., including fingers, feet, clothes, hair

_ make symbols of houses or apartments to enclose people. *Be sure to observe the chimney position and direction (vertical, horizontal). Some teachers have noted a correlation between the chimney position and the emergent writer: when the chimney is represented in a perpendicular form, children can generally use simple print. (See top of next page.)*

__ add recognizable symbols of other familiar objects in the environment, such as trees, flowers
__ add many more details

__ use a variety of tools to create different moods/impressions, e.g., chalk for snow, outline of a shape for effect
__ make pictures that have a base line and a sky line
__ create pictures that have a recognizable story

__ use different illustrative techniques such as cartoons, flaps, borders
__ make pictures that show profiles, relative size, perspectives

The Ways That Children Use the Materials for Writing

They might:

___ make marks to imitate text in English or other first languages

___ use circles and lines to tell stories

___ attempt to make letters, usually capitals from their own name

David

___ print random letters in a scattered fashion over their picture or blank page, often using those in their own name

___ print random letters in a more organized form, e.g., vertical or horizontal

___ print random letters which imitate text, e.g., going left to right

___ begin to match sound and symbol by labelling details in their pictures. They often use the strongest sound in the word.

____ use more than one sound for a word, usually strong consonants such as *s*, *c*, and *t* and long vowels

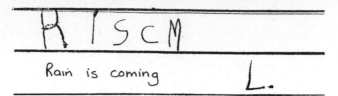

____ use more letters accurately
____ use spaces or dots or lines to show the difference between a word and a letter

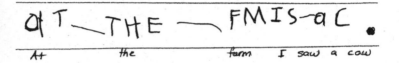

____ add captions to their pictures

____ use both capital and small letters
____ incorporate some familiar sight words, e.g., "mommy," a friend's name
____ incorporate some repetitive function words such as "the" and "is"

— use more accurate spellings

— add punctuation, e.g., periods, question marks, quotation marks
— use capital letters in appropriate places

Winnie The Pooh is Sitting in Front of His House on The Log.

— use writing structures, such as sentences, paragraphs, chapters
— use different forms, such as dialogue, question, and answer
— write in a different genre ranging from captions, lists, directions, an interview, a story, poetry

The Way That Children Show an Interest in Drawing or Writing

They might:

__ choose the writing/drawing centre

__ draw and write at other centres, e.g., draw a flag to add to their block structure

__ choose the computer

__ share their work with a friend or teacher when asked

__ spontaneously share their work with a friend, teacher or family member

__ ask to share their work with the group

__ share their work in a larger setting, e.g., in the library or in another class

__ write or draw several pieces about the same topic

__ begin to collate writing and illustrations, e.g., putting all the stories about the sea together

__ continue to work on a piece of writing or a drawing for more than one work period

__ revisit a piece of writing/drawing

__ ask to display or publish favorite pieces of work

__ begin to edit work with support and reminders

__ willingly edit their work, incorporating their knowledge of illustrations, grammar, punctuation and spelling

__ independently edit and revise their work, applying new knowledge

__ publish favorite pieces (drawings or writing) using publishing techniques

These developmental mileposts are guidelines only and are not intended to be all-inclusive or prescriptive.

7/The Sand Centre

Why a Sand Centre Is Needed in a MAG Classroom

Sand is a medium that seems to appeal to all children universally. They come to it naturally from early childhood. Even very young children gain satisfaction and success when using sand. It appeals to their senses. It is soothing and feels good to the touch. It is intriguing and extends their curiosity and creativity.

The sand centre is a place where children can explore many mathematical, scientific and technological concepts. Work in the sand allows children to explore these concepts in a hands-on way, providing the foundation for later abstract thinking. In addition, it develops eye-hand coordination and small muscle control. Its very nature fascinates children. It invites exploration, experimentation and problem solving.

Activities at this centre also provide meaningful opportunities for language development. The children acquire new vocabulary. They build new knowledge, skills and values by talking, listening, reading, writing, cooperating, experimenting, dramatizing and observing.

Exploring Hands On

In our MAG classrooms the children were motivated naturally by the example of the more sophisticated users of sand. The children were always seeing new behaviors to imitate.

Experimentation and investigation flourished in this atmosphere where they were expected, but not pressured, to explore.

At this centre many informal demonstrations took place. The more sophisticated users willingly and naturally answered the questions of newcomers, questions such as "Where does this belong?" or "How do I get more water to make a lake?" They supported new learners in their efforts in the same way that new learners are supported in a family setting. These more competent learners gained satisfaction, confidence, and self-assurance and consolidated their own new understandings.

Materials That Encourage Learning at the Sand Centre in a MAG Classroom

Here are some materials useful at the sand centre:

- commercial and found materials of varying sizes to accommodate the different degrees of grip and control of children of different ages and stages of development, e.g., kitchen utensils, garden tools
- props, e.g., miniature animals, people, dinosaurs
- materials from the natural environment such as rocks, twigs, and shells
- materials to extend children's explorations, e.g., magnifying glasses, scales, measurement containers, sieves, funnels, string, rope and pulleys, books and other reference materials
- materials for recording, including pencils, graph paper, post-its, clipboard, pieces of acrylic with overhead markers for writing
- materials for clean-up, such as a dustpan, small and large brooms and brushes

In a single-age/grade classroom we always began with no tools because we wanted the children to explore the properties of both wet and dry sand. As we observed the children in their use of the sand, we added materials and tools that would enable the children to continue to develop concepts and skills. For example, to help them develop an understanding of volume, we added bowls of different sizes and shapes. We introduced these materials slowly, so the children would be familiar with the expected routines and not feel overwhelmed by the wide choice.

In our MAG classrooms, more materials were available right from the beginning of the school year due to the range of interest, experience and competence. Tools for digging, burying, filling, pouring, sifting, measuring, moulding, scraping, and constructing were stored in labelled bins. To encourage dramatic play we included many props, such as cars, trucks, planes, multi-racial models of people, animals, twigs, string, cardboard, and dishes for water. Markers, cardboard, cards, pencils, and clipboards were also available for the children to use for recording. The children selected the materials they needed to complete their work. Other children, as well as the teacher, made suggestions to extend the learning.

The Sand Centre in a MAG Classroom:
Some Questions for the Reflective Practitioner to Ask
if an Environment for Success Is to Be Created

1. How do I ensure that the sand centre is safe?
   - Ensure that the sand the children are using meets safety standards. In other words, avoid sand that is high in silica content.
   - Discuss the chosen location with the caretaking staff.
   - Introduce children to the routines and expectations for the centre. For example, you will want regular sweeping to reduce slipping.
   - Regularly check the materials for breakage or damage.
   - Discuss with the children how many people can safely use this centre. The number will vary depending on the size of the sandbox and space available.
   - Ensure that the sandbox is within your hearing and sight or that of other adults.

2. How do I ensure that this centre remains inviting and challenging to children of more than one age and stage of development?
   - You could introduce materials for different purposes, digging, pouring, moulding, moving, sifting, measuring, recording, and so on.
   - Regularly add more materials which extend the concepts with which the children are experimenting, e.g., measurement cups and spoons.
   - Reorganize the storage of the materials used to date so that the shapes of new materials can be *outlined* on a table or shelf.
   - You could group materials into labelled baskets/boxes according to their purpose, ranging from moulding or pouring to serving as props for dramatic play.

3. What is my role as teacher at the sand centre in a MAG classroom?
   - You could observe individuals and small groups of children as they work.
   - You could keep a record of your observations.
   - Be available to extend the learning. Sit with, listen to, answer questions, and generally interact with the children.
   - Twin children of differing ages and stages.
   - Direct children to their peers for information and help.
   - Ensure that the materials are appropriate and well maintained.
   - Provide materials that extend the learning.

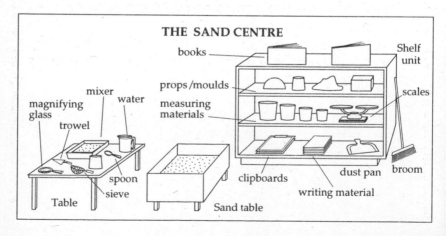

THE SAND CENTRE

Some Mileposts to Help Guide Teacher Observations of Children Working in the Sand in a MAG Classroom

The Skills That Children Demonstrate

They might:

__ feel the sand, let it run through their fingers
__ move the sand
__ pat the sand
__ mould the sand
__ dig in the sand
__ bury objects in the sand
__ use tools with control to scrape, pat, move, dig
__ pour from one container to another
__ pour from one container to another with control
__ fill containers with control
__ use other materials to move sand, e.g., funnels, spoons, scoops, pulleys
__ compare amounts of sand — more, less
__ use other non-standard materials to compare quantity, e.g., containers of different sizes
__ use standardized materials to measure, e.g., graduated containers, simple scales, measuring spoons
__ make signs to label their work
__ write narrative or expository text to describe and retell
__ record discoveries and results of simple experiments
__ refer to books/photographs/videos for information and ideas
__ apply new knowledge to other situations, e.g., add water appropriately based on learning from past experiences

The Knowledge That Children Demonstrate

They might:

__ recognize the different properties of sand

__ recognize the possibilities for the uses of different tools

__ use appropriate language to describe, question, predict, estimate, direct, compare, draw conclusions

__ explore new mathematical and scientific concepts, e.g., volume, mass, cause and effect

__ use their imaginations to create a landscape

__ add props to a landscape for dramatic play

The Ways That Children Show Their Interest in Sand

They might:

__ voluntarily choose sand as an activity

__ willingly experiment and explore the properties of sand

__ use a variety of tools

__ concentrate for a reasonable length of time

__ willingly take risks. For example: "Let's see what happens when we add more water."

__ share the materials

__ work alone

__ work side by side with other children, sharing the equipment

__ work cooperatively, sharing and taking turns and exchanging ideas

__ work collaboratively with other students, planning and implementing a shared idea or project

__ follow routines

__ accept responsibility for their own behavior

__ accept suggestions from other children and adults

__ show leadership by helping other children to solve problems and tidy up

These developmental mileposts are guidelines only and are not intended to be all-inclusive or prescriptive.

8/The Water Centre

Why a Water Centre Is Needed in a MAG Classroom

Water, like sand, is a medium that all children instinctively find appealing. It intrigues them, appeals to their senses, and is soothing to their touch. As a result, most children from an early age take delight in splashing in puddles, running through the hose, and blowing bubbles. Once children are acclimatized to the feel of water, bath time for most of them becomes a time of great enjoyment and learning. They naturally splash and move their toys through the water, manipulating and exploring its properties. Through the unstructured play in the home, children begin to experiment with and learn about the properties of water.

Exploring Mathematical, Scientific and Technological Concepts

In the classroom, the water centre builds on children's natural interest. The centre becomes a place where such mathematical, scientific and technological concepts as flotation, measurement, and displacement are explored and understood. By exploring these concepts in a hands-on way children develop a sound basis for further abstract thinking. Activities in the water provide opportunities for them to develop eye-hand coordination and small muscle control. The very nature of water invites the children to explore, experiment and problem-solve.

This centre is rich in opportunities for the children to learn and use the language of mathematics, science and technology.

They acquire new vocabulary, make predictions, test their hypotheses and share their findings. The children learn to record their findings in a logical, scientific manner. By talking, listening, writing, cooperating, experimenting and observing, they develop critical mathematical, scientific and technological skills, knowledge and values.

In single-grade classrooms, teachers often first open this centre with only water and clean-up materials. Doing so provides the children with lots of opportunities to explore and experiment, unhampered by the constraints of specific tools. And we found it helpful to follow this practice even in our MAG classrooms.

However, we went beyond that. We stored a small quantity of tools in basins near the water table. We encouraged those children who had more prior experience with this medium to set their own challenges, verbalize these challenges, and then with our help, select those tools that would help them solve these problems. For example: "I want to find out if all plastic things like mine sink." As all the children gained in experience we carefully added selected materials, such as those that float and sink. Doing this helped the children to focus on specific scientific concepts.

In this kind of MAG atmosphere, the example of the more sophisticated users of water motivated other children to experiment. The teacher made many informal demonstrations at this centre. Someone was always available to answer questions, offer a helping hand at tidy up or share the problem solving. **The younger children learned a lot by imitating the behaviors and language of the more sophisticated water users.** On the other hand, these more experienced learners consolidated their own understandings by explaining, describing and sharing their knowledge. Together, children of all levels of competence made predictions, solved problems and shared their findings.

Materials That Encourage Learning at the Water Centre in a MAG Classroom

The following are useful:

- a large water table that is in good repair
- materials to help tidy up: sponges, bucket
- containers that have spouts of different shapes for pouring
- containers for measuring, standard and non-standard form
- basters, eye droppers of different sizes
- funnels of different sizes
- water wheels both homemade and commercial
- containers with holes of different sizes at different levels to explore water pressure
- disposable straws instead of tubing for health reasons
- instruments to change the state of the water, e.g., egg beaters, paddles
- materials to add to the water to change its state, e.g., food coloring, soap, salt, snow, ice
- paper weights to observe movement of liquids
- sponges of different sizes, natural and manufactured
- materials that sink and float
- paper, graph paper, acetate, plastic clipboards for recording information
- pencils, waterproof markers, rulers for recording
- books to provide more information about the properties of water, to help inform the predictions

---

Bubbles

Ingredients
2 cups warm water
6 tablespoons glycerine (from drugstore)
6 tablespoons liquid detergent
Dash of sugar

Bubbles can be made by mixing the above ingredients.

The Water Centre in a MAG Classroom: Some Questions for the Reflective Practitioner to Ask if an Environment for Success Is to Be Created

1. How do I ensure that the water centre is safe?
   - Introduce children to the routines and expectations for the centre. For example, regular mopping will reduce slipping.
   - Change the water daily.
   - Keep the temperature of the water comfortable.
   - Regularly wash the equipment with a mild disinfectant.
   - Regularly check the materials for breakage or damage.
   - Consider health issues when adding equipment; be sure to remind children not to put any equipment in their mouths or to drink the water.
   - Discuss with the children how many people can safely use this centre.
   - Ensure that the water table is within your hearing and sight or that of other adults.

2. How do I ensure that tidy up is successful and that the children take responsibility for it?
   - You could organize the materials in labelled bins or baskets.
   - Arrange these storage containers on marked shelves or on a table near the water table.
   - Introduce and remove the materials as necessary to avoid clutter and disorganization.
   - Establish clear expectations for clean-up.

3. What is my role as the teacher at the water centre in a MAG classroom?
   - Ensure that this centre is exciting and vibrant. Add surprises — change the color of the water, add a collection of found materials that sink and float.
   - Be sure to develop a schedule for observing a manageable number of children as they work at the water centre.
   - Plan so that adults are available to listen to the children, make observations, answer the children's questions and pose new questions to extend the learning.

- You might twin children of different ages and stages.
- Direct children to their peers for information and help.
- Regularly introduce materials/equipment which can motivate or help the children solve their inquiries.
- Maintain health standards.

4. How might I ensure that the children and their parents see the water centre as valuable as other activities such as reading and writing?
   - You could timetable the centre as part of a math/science/technology period.
   - Be sure to have the water table inside the classroom; resist having it in the hallway.
   - Schedule adult time in the centre so that you, a co-op student or a parent can observe and interact with the children.
   - Share important discoveries with the class either during the work period or at its end.
   - Keep the centre alive, challenging and well maintained.
   - Include samples (photographs and simple recordings) in the children's portfolios for reporting.
   - Inform parents about the importance of the learning in the water — take photographs and display the range of expertise.
   - Hold a parents' night to share the purpose for the centre and the range of learning that occurs: from simple pouring to complex ordering of containers according to volume.

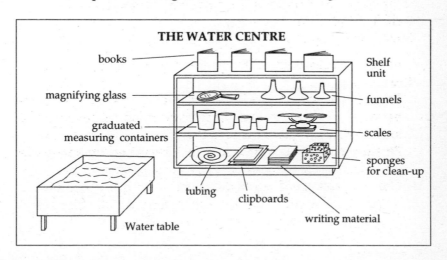

THE WATER CENTRE

books — Shelf unit

magnifying glass — funnels

graduated measuring containers — scales

tubing

clipboards

sponges for clean-up

writing material

Water table

Some Mileposts to Help Guide Teacher Observations of Children Working in the Water in a MAG Classroom

The Skills That Children Demonstrate

They might:

___ feel the water, let it run through their fingers

___ move the water — splash, drag their hands through it

___ pat the water to make different splashes

___ move objects through and under the water

___ move water from one container to another

___ use other materials to move water: funnels, spoons, scoops, basters

___ pour water from one container to another with more control

___ recognize when a container is empty or almost full

___ fill containers with control and accuracy

___ recognize quantities of water — more, less, same

___ use other non-standard materials to compare quantity, that is, containers of different sizes

___ use standardized materials to measure: graduated containers, simple scales, measuring spoons

___ experiment with the concepts of sinking and floating

___ add materials to water to change its feel and look: soap, salt

___ change the properties of water — heat it, freeze it

___ make signs to label their work

___ write narrative or expository text to describe their work and retell what they did

___ record discoveries and results of simple experiments

___ refer to books/photographs/videos for information and ideas

___ apply new knowledge to other situations. For example, if the children had been following a recipe where accurate measurement was necessary, in the water centre they would apply this new learning in more standard measurement by pouring water more carefully and using standard measures.

The Knowledge That Children Demonstrate

They might:

___ use appropriate props in the water to support dramatic play, perhaps adding boats as they role-play

___ recognize how water and its properties can be changed with the addition of different materials. For example: Salt makes the water more buoyant.

___ recognize the possibilities for the uses of different tools, e.g., water wheel, funnel

___ use appropriate language to describe, question, predict, estimate, direct, compare, draw conclusions

___ explore new mathematical and scientific concepts such as volume, flotation, displacement, water pressure

The Ways That Children Show Their Interest in Water

They might:

___ voluntarily choose water as an activity

___ willingly experiment and explore the properties of water

___ use a variety of tools

___ concentrate for a reasonable length of time

___ willingly take risks. For example: "Let's see what happens when we add salt to the water."

___ work alone

___ work side by side with other children, sharing the equipment

___ work cooperatively, sharing and taking turns and exchanging ideas

___ work independently (alone or in groups) to identify a problem, create a hypothesis, design experiments and record the results, such as the discovery that water seeks its own level

___ accept responsibility for their own behavior

___ show leadership by helping other children to solve problems and tidy up

These developmental mileposts are guidelines only and are not intended to be all-inclusive or prescriptive.

9/Interest Centres

Why Interest Centres Are Needed in a MAG Classroom

Interest centres are temporary centres which evolve from the children's interests. They are often initiated by a story, special event, question, news item, field trip, video or home activity. They tend to begin as individual collections, and as other children show interest, evolve into a mini interest centre. For some, the interest becomes broader, appealing to many of the children in the room.

Teachers can capitalize on these interests and use them as vehicles to introduce a variety of skills, knowledge and attitudes. Interest centres allow teachers to plan in an integrated way. Many of the activities involve reading, writing, listening, speaking, viewing, representing, problem solving, graphing, numeracy, patterning, measuring, dramatizing, singing, playing instruments, drawing, painting, creating, building, observing, exploring, testing hypotheses and drawing conclusions as well as other learning experiences.

Reflecting Greater Diversity in Children's Interests and Competencies

Interest centres, since they are so closely connected to the current expressed interests of the children, change frequently and vary in duration. They can include collections of real objects, artifacts, props, models, related books, puzzles, and posters.

In a MAG classroom, the children's interests and competencies are more diverse. As a result, there should be opportunities for several interest centres to develop at one time. The centres will vary in intensity and scope, depending on how many children are interested.

Mini interest centres and individual collections are present in a MAG classroom at the same time. We do not expect all of the children to participate in any one centre. Rather, we encourage them to pursue their own special projects based on their personal, relevant interests or inquiries. No child is ever forced to pursue activities at an interest centre.

Benefiting from the Presence of Experts

Interest centres are particularly necessary and beneficial in MAG classrooms.

The younger children have the benefit of observing more competent learners as they refer to books for information, record ideas and problem-solve. They have the advantage of being a part of an exciting and challenging environment. They are exposed to the vocabulary, ideas, and suggestions of more experienced learners. **Older children have a captive audience. They can consolidate their learning by describing, presenting and sharing the results of their inquiries with their younger classmates. They gain enormous satisfaction by sharing their skills and knowledge.** In the MAG classroom, many experts and coaches are available to offer information and directions about specific interests.

Teachers need to resist the temptation to impose or introduce new interest centres which may not interest the children. In traditional settings, they often seem to impose interests through contrived themes such as winter, summer, color, fall, apples. In our view, themes such as these cannot generate genuine interest centres: they assume that the topic will motivate all children at the same time in the same manner. Rarely does this happen. When we taught in MAG classrooms, we focused always on the skills, knowledge and attitudes that the children were expected to acquire and not on the specific narrow content of a theme.

We found that capitalizing on the children's interests was more beneficial than covering specific content. The children could develop the prescribed skills, knowledge and attitudes regardless of the content. For example, if the desired outcome is that the children learn to read with understanding, the theme or topic is irrelevant to the teacher. In fact, we have confirmed that children must consider the task relevant and take responsibility for the choice of topic, if authentic and lifelong learning is to occur.

Developing Research Skills

Interest centres and personal inquiries allow children to begin to develop basic research skills. They learn to devise their own questions and to use many resources to find the answers. They become adept at developing questions instead of answering the teacher's questions. **The varied interests of both younger and older children help to create a stimulating and exciting environment where they can share their skills, knowledge and attitudes.**

Materials That Encourage Learning at an Interest Centre

The following represent a wide range of materials:

- collections of materials at a variety of developmental levels
- concrete objects/real items, e.g., shells, nets, lobster trap
- semi-abstract materials: pictures, posters, models
- abstract materials: books, videos, CDs, activities, puzzles
- round tables to display materials
- small tables where the children can work
- bulletin board for displaying pictures, posters and children's work
- bias-free materials that reflect a variety of races, cultures and gender roles
- materials such as magnifying glasses, scales, and measuring tapes to extend the inquiries
- writing materials: pencils, markers, graph paper, clipboard

The Interest Centres in a MAG Classroom: Some Questions for the Reflective Practitioner to Ask if an Environment for Success Is to Be Created

1. How can I ensure that the tidy up is successful and that the children take responsibility for it?
   - You could outline a place for each item at the centre, so it is easy to tidy up and to notice if anything is missing.
   - Group the materials according to use for easy access, e.g., put all the books together.
   - Encourage the children to take the materials to permanent centres, such as the writing or visual arts, to work.
   - Encourage the children to work at the centre to explore some of the materials.
   - Encourage the children to remove some of the materials to use on the floor or nearby tables. They might do this with board games or building materials, for example.

2. How can I ensure that the interest centres interest and challenge children of more than one age and stage of development?
   - Be sure to provide a range of materials at a variety of developmental levels.
   - Add something for everyone. For example, you could provide real objects or materials to manipulate; materials for matching, comparing, relating and making connections to the real world (pictures, models); abstract materials for reference and extending the interest; and materials for recording findings and ideas.
   - Close the centre whenever the interest wanes.
   - Introduce new materials slowly and regularly to extend and stimulate thinking.
   - Feature a few small interest centres at one time rather than one all-consuming theme.
   - Display the children's work in interesting ways, perhaps hanging it from the ceiling.

3. What is the role of the teacher at an interest centre in a MAG classroom?
   - Schedule time for the teacher and adults to listen to and observe the children to determine relevant interests.
   - Highlight and expand, where appropriate, individual collections that seem to attract the interest of a small group of children.
   - Make suggestions (not dictates) about the development of new centres and the closing of others.
   - Involve and encourage the children to create a new collection or interest centre.
   - Collect materials that are bias free and safe to use.
   - Introduce new materials slowly.
   - Introduce related materials and activities to expand the interest to other children at other levels of development.
   - Make connections between the children's various collections. Note, for example, that cats and dogs are part of a wider category, pets.
   - Schedule time to visit each interest centre to observe the learning and interactions of the children.
   - Schedule time to extend the learning. You might do so to add new resource materials, to set challenges, or to suggest ways to record information.
   - Set aside time to meet regularly with the librarian, to plan and access new materials that support the children's investigations.

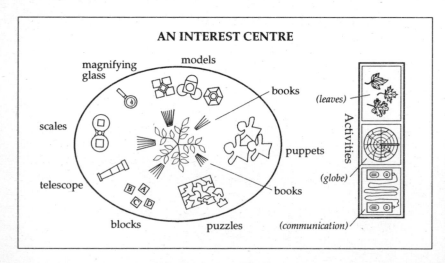

AN INTEREST CENTRE

Some Mileposts to Help Guide Teacher Observations of Children Working at Interest Centres in a MAG Classroom

The Skills That Children Demonstrate
They might:
__ talk with others and ask questions about the materials
__ use models or pictures as references
__ use a variety of techniques to answer their questions, including asking another child or an adult
__ look at books, videos and CDs for information
__ make connections with other interests
__ respond to the materials in many ways, including drawing, painting, building, dramatizing, telling stories
__ record information in different forms, perhaps through pictures, labels, simple text
__ apply new knowledge in other situations

The Knowledge That Children Demonstrate
They might:
__ learn about the real world, e.g., plants, bugs, pets
__ access information in a variety of ways, such as reading, listening, viewing
__ sort, classify and record information in several ways, e.g., pictures, tallies, graphs
__ report and share information in a number of ways, such as talking, drawing, charting

The Interest That Children Show in the Interest Centres
They might:
__ become interested in the collections of others
__ add to the interest centres or collections in the room, e.g., by bringing in a shell
__ initiate new collections, bringing in rocks, for example
__ persevere until questions are answered

These developmental mileposts are guidelines only and are not intended to be all-inclusive or prescriptive.

10/The Construction Materials Centre

Why Construction Materials Are Needed in a MAG Classroom

Children naturally begin to construct using materials readily available in their environment. Toddlers intuitively manipulate, stack and sort cardboard boxes, lids, pots and pans, plastic food containers and nesting toys. We can observe them exploring many basic mathematical, scientific and technological concepts even at this young age.

Teachers need to promote the development of these concepts. To do so, they must provide many opportunities in school for children to continue to build. The introduction of particular materials, both found and commercial, leads children to consolidate and extend their knowledge and problem-solving abilities.

By exploring and experimenting with a variety of construction materials, children develop intellectually, emotionally, socially and physically. As teachers observe children and introduce new materials, the children learn to sort, order, count, compare, classify, pose questions, problem-solve and draw conclusions. They can also develop an understanding of other mathematical, scientific and technological concepts, such as number, pattern, measurement, geometry, bridging, balance, and energy. Teachers use construction activities to teach children how to record such information in a number of ways, including pictorial or written reports, tallies, graphs, and surveys. For example, a child might write "I used 27 blue blocks when I built my tower" or draw a picture of the structure.

Construction materials also provide an excellent vehicle for children to acquire and use language. Children have many opportunities to speak, listen, read, write, view and represent. They learn to use language to describe, direct, report, retell, question and resolve conflicts. They are also exposed to specific mathematical, scientific and technological vocabulary: this blue block is *equal* to two small yellow blocks; this floor *area* is bigger than that floor area. Working with many commercial and found materials leads children to explore the arts instinctively, creating, imagining, dramatizing and expressing themselves. They learn to represent their ideas using symbols for the real object: a thin, long block becomes a bridge.

Discovering Many Ways to Explore

Construction materials can be used in a variety of ways at a variety of developmental levels. There is no one way to use them, and children at every age and stage can use them with success. As a result, the learning experience is non-threatening and invites children to take risks; it builds self-confidence and develops their self-esteem.

The materials allow children to work independently or in co-operation and collaboration with others. What varies is their choice, the teacher's goals and their levels of social development. Social skills, such as sharing, interacting with others, and working cooperatively and collaboratively, are developed. The unique nature of the materials also ensures that important physical skills, such as eye-hand coordination, balance, and large- and small-muscle control, are developed naturally.

Learning through construction materials is particularly successful in MAG classrooms. **Children constantly see different ways to use the materials.** They see some children who are simply exploring the materials while others are testing simple hypotheses and recording the results. The environment is exciting and stimulating. In such an atmosphere, children naturally imitate, question, seek help and share their results. The teacher has ample opportunity to demonstrate new learning. The children are the experts and act as coaches and tutors.

Materials That Encourage Learning with Construction Materials

Certain materials in the environment lend themselves to the development of particular mathematical, scientific and technological concepts. Teachers in MAG classrooms need to collect a wide range of stackable materials of uniform size and shape to help permit this development. They should store these materials in individually labelled containers, perhaps baskets or bins.

The following found materials have proven successful and lend themselves to the development of specific math/science/technology concepts:

- corks, yarn spools
- beer bungs, both plain and colored
- film containers
- lipstick lids and lids from other containers
- varying sizes of plastic cups
- cardboard boxes
- margarine/yogurt containers
- plastic bottles

The following commercial materials are useful in the development of a number of math/science/technology concepts. Teachers need to observe their children carefully to determine which materials might be added to encourage further exploration. Some of the materials lend themselves to the development of particular skills. For example: In addition to pattern blocks, Towerifics, Jigantiks, and Formations lend themselves to the development of patterning concepts. Similarly, base ten, Unifix cubes, corks, and bungs invite the exploration of number, perimeter, area and balance. Zaks, Polydrons, and geometric shapes help motivate children to explore geometry. Kapla, spools, Unifix blocks, Cuisenaire rods, and Lazy are examples of materials that help children to experiment with measurement.

Here are some examples of successful commercial materials:

- plain and colored blocks, large and small
- pattern blocks
- base ten blocks — Unifix blocks
- Cuisenaire rods
- Kapla
- Duplo
- Lazy
- Jigantiks
- Towerifics
- Ringamagics
- Formations
- Zaks
- Sonos
- Polydrons
- Ramagon
- Struts
- geometric shapes, 2D and 3D

Here are some examples of successful props for constructions:

- counters — cars, trucks, farm animals, teddy bears
- found materials — stones, pine cones, shells, twigs, feathers
- colored disks

The Construction Materials Centre in a MAG Classroom: Some Questions for the Reflective Practitioner to Ask if an Environment for Success Is to Be Created

1. What is the role of the teacher?
   - Schedule time to visit the construction centre on a regular basis, so that you can observe and track the children's progress.
   - Use appropriate vocabulary to help extend the children's mathematical, scientific and technological language.
   - Ensure that materials are used in a safe and appropriate manner.
   - Collect samples of children's work, perhaps taking photographs.
   - Provide materials for children to record results of their work, perhaps a math notebook, clipboard, or graph paper.

- Introduce new materials to extend observed learning or to teach new concepts.
- Offer specific challenges to allow children to restate their learning, make connections with other learning, reflect on what they have learned and pose new questions.
- Offer relevant and appropriate mini-lessons to students who need support.
- Communicate regularly with parents to explain the learning with construction materials.
- Share and celebrate children's efforts and discoveries.

2. How do I ensure that the children and their parents see working with construction materials as valuable as reading and writing?
   - Timetable building as part of a math/science/technology period or give building equal status on the timetable. In that way even those students who are reluctant will have to use the materials.
   - Resist the temptation to have children build only when their traditionally "real" paper and pencil work is done. *Kindergarten teachers in many areas still think "real learning" occurs only in teacher-directed, product-oriented activities, for example, matching numbers to numerals on a sheet. They see work in construction materials, also in sand and water, as something to occupy some of the children while they get on with the "real" classroom work with a few children.*
   - Schedule adult time (teacher, co-op student, parent) in the centre to observe and interact with the children. Once teachers do this themselves and meet with other teachers to share their observations, they become advocates. They often can't readily see the learning because their own knowledge of math/science/technology concepts is not as deep as it is for language skills.
   - Record observations of children as they work. Schedule a manageable number of no more than four to observe each day.
   - Keep the centre alive, challenging and well maintained. Adding new materials such as string, cardboard, tinfoil, sticks, pulleys and props, such as small people and cars, will help achieve this.

- Include samples (photographs and simple recordings) in the children's portfolios.
- Inform parents about the learning that occurs when children construct; take photographs and display the range of expertise.
- Organize a parent night to share with parents the purpose for the centre and the range of learning that occurs, e.g., from simple stacking to complex balancing or patterning.

3. How do I ensure that the materials are easily accessible?
   - You could provide a number of spaces where these materials can be used: on tables, on the floor, on Plexiglas supported between two blocks so that children can view constructions from many angles.
   - You could provide opportunities for children to construct independently or with others.
   - Provide an appropriate amount of space: big blocks require more space than other materials.
   - Determine how this centre will be used in relation to other centres and locate it accordingly, perhaps near a dramatic play centre for additional props or the visual arts centre for materials to create props.
   - Determine the number of children that can work at the centre safely and productively.

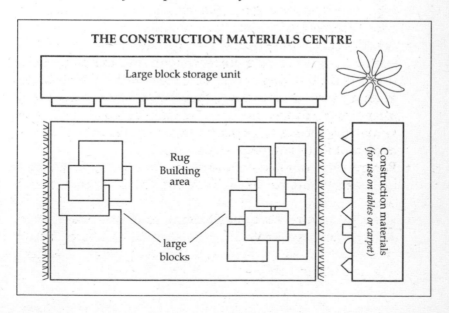

THE CONSTRUCTION MATERIALS CENTRE

Large block storage unit

Rug Building area

large blocks

Construction materials
(for use on tables or carpet)

Some Mileposts to Help Guide Teacher Observations of Children Working with Construction Materials in a MAG Classroom

The Ways That Children Use Construction Materials
They might:
__ randomly move the materials from one place to another
__ stack the materials and then knock them down
__ purposefully make towers, using a few of the materials
__ connect towers and other structures
__ use the materials to make an enclosure
__ make recognizable structures

The Number and Numeracy Skills That Children Demonstrate When Using Construction Materials
They might:
__ sort the materials into groups
__ order the materials
__ count the materials in their structure by rote
__ count small groups of materials they have used with one-to-one correspondence, e.g., point to each block and count accurately
__ classify materials according to color, shape, object, and so on
__ estimate and check their guesses of the number of materials used
__ recognize sets of numbers to 10
__ count by 2's, 5's, 10's
__ understand the concepts of more than, less than, and same as
__ recognize one more than, one less than a number of objects
__ record by writing numerals
__ explore the concepts of addition and subtraction
__ explore the concepts of simple fractions

The Skills in Geometry That Children Demonstrate When Using Construction Materials

They might:

__ build shapes

__ use simple vocabulary to describe their structures, e.g., behind, beside, on top of

__ classify/sort materials according to shape

__ explain the rule they used to classify/sort

__ identify geometric shapes in their structures and environment, e.g., recognizing a house as a square

__ accurately name the geometric shapes

__ represent geometric shapes, perhaps with other materials, with a picture or with print

__ recognize symmetry

The Data Management and Probability Skills That Children Demonstrate When They Use Construction Materials

They might:

__ collect/sort materials

__ return the props to their appropriate container, putting all the pigs back in the animal container, for example

__ use vocabulary to describe how they have organized the materials

__ record information using pictures, numbers, shapes, words, tallies, simple graphs

__ predict what might happen to their structures. For example: "If I take any off from this side, it will fall."

__ construct according to an idea: "I'm going to make a farm with lots of fields for the different animals."

__ construct according to a preconceived plan, perhaps drawn or written

The Measurement Skills That Children Demonstrate When Using Construction Materials

They might:

__ explore the concept of measurement, e.g., long, short

__ use measurement vocabulary, e.g., light, heavy

__ compare measurements, e.g., quantities — full, empty

___ order the materials according to measurement, e.g., small to big
___ use non-standard materials to measure
___ estimate. For example: "My tower is 4 hands tall."
___ explore perimeter, e.g., make fences and other enclosures
___ explore volume, e.g., fill containers with materials
___ explore area, e.g., cover a large block with small blocks
___ explore mass. For example: "The big blocks are heavier than the small blocks."

The Patterning Skills That Children Demonstrate When Using Construction Materials

They might:
___ understand the difference between a pattern, such as stripes or dots, and no pattern
___ recognize simple patterns in the environment, such as on their clothes
___ point out patterns, such as color and shape, in their structures
___ create their own patterns using the materials
___ use vocabulary to describe patterns
___ copy patterns
___ extend patterns
___ record the patterns they have made using different attributes, e.g., shape, color, size, number

The Problem-Solving Skills That Children Demonstrate When They Use Construction Materials

They might:
___ identify a problem/difficulty with their structure
___ experiment with a variety of materials and solutions
___ realize that problems may have more than one possible solution
___ ask for help from the teacher or peers when they have a problem. For example: "My bridge keeps breaking. I need help."
___ persist until they find a solution to their problem
___ look for alternative solutions
___ describe the problem and the solution they discovered
___ record their problem-solving experiences through pictures, charts, lists, and so on

The Scientific and Technological Skills That Children Demonstrate When They Use Construction Materials

They might:

__ make observations. For example: "It's hard to build a bridge. Mine keeps falling down."

__ ask questions, such as "Why does it keep falling down?"

__ identify problems. For example: "I think there are not enough blocks on the sides to hold it up."

__ make predictions about possible outcomes and solutions. "Maybe if I put more blocks on the sides or a longer bit underneath, it will stay up."

__ use simple tools and materials to test hypotheses. "Maybe I'll try a board from the big blocks or a piece of cardboard."

__ describe their observations and make interpretations in order to generalize. For example: "The cardboard didn't work — it was too soft. The board was too heavy. The blocks all fell down. I think I need a skinnier, smaller board."

__ draw conclusions. For example: "If the bridge part is too heavy, the whole thing just collapses."

The Methods of Recording That Children Use

They might:

__ draw a picture about what they have made

__ organize pictures of their work in a book

__ write about what they built

__ record specific features of what they have created in terms of pattern, balance, geometry, measurement. For example: A younger child might say, "This wall is taller than this one" while an older child might write such an observation down.

__ have a plan for what they are going to construct

__ create a plan, in written or pictorial form, to show what they intend to build

The Ways That Children Show an Interest in Construction Materials

They might:

__ choose to build

__ show confidence when building. For example: "I can make a garage like my dad's."

__ take risks, perhaps trying new materials

__ build for increasingly longer periods of time

__ volunteer to share their work

__ respond when asked about their work

__ share their expertise, that is, help other classmates

__ record their work willingly

These developmental mileposts are guidelines only and are not intended to be all-inclusive or prescriptive.

11/The Home Centre and Extensions

Why a Home Centre with Extensions Is Needed in a MAG Classroom

In MAG classrooms, the home centre is a vehicle through which children can explore their world and make sense of experiences, relationships, feelings and everyday events. This centre is of critical importance in the emotional, intellectual and social growth of each child. It is equally important as children grow older. As children mature, they need the healthy outlet that such a centre provides to explore their emotions and fears. Their concerns, problems, and reactions do not disappear, but become more complex.

By exploring familiar and imaginary roles, children gain a deeper understanding of everyday experiences, for example, the arrival of a baby in the family. They have many opportunities to sort out their actions and reactions and to rehearse their responses to past and upcoming events, such as a visit to the hairdresser. As children role-play, they learn to take risks in familiar, supportive settings, and in doing so, build their self-confidence and self-esteem.

They also develop language in a natural, personal and meaningful way. We used the home centre and other extensions of this centre to introduce the children to literacy in relevant and exciting ways; for example, environmental print. The children had many authentic reasons to speak, listen, read, write, view and represent. These might include reading a menu when ordering a meal in a restaurant, writing a prescription for a patient, talking on the phone to a friend and looking through an album of baby pictures.

The centre provided a familiar context in which children could problem-solve in a meaningful way: "How many places do we need to set at the table?" and so on. They could explore concepts in mathematics, science, and technology in a natural and relevant manner, perhaps considering recycling. Children use their imaginations and creativity to express themselves. Their dramatic play is not a performance — they truly live the experience.

Strengthening Social Development Naturally

As the children work in this centre, they experience many natural situations in which they can develop social relationships. They learn to share the materials, take turns and develop strategies that help them solve conflicts effectively. When adding new materials, we purposefully created situations which made it necessary for the children to share and develop other social skills: one example is offering fewer dolls than children.

In the MAG classroom, this centre naturally lent itself to many different extensions. As the children had experiences beyond their homes, they extended their role play to include experiences from the broader community. As a result, **extensions such as a dentist's office, a store, or a fire station occurred more frequently with the presence of older, more experienced learners.** Older children exposed younger children to more sophisticated emotional, intellectual and social development levels. In turn, the older children could practise new knowledge, skills and attitudes.

Materials That Encourage Learning in the Home Centre in a MAG Classroom

When selecting materials for the home centre, we were careful to be inclusive. We ensured that all the items were bias free in terms of race, age, gender, and culture and represented a variety of family structures; we strove to make the materials relevant to the children's lives. We were also careful to ensure that the materials represented the broader community and global village. One good example is lengths of cloth for use as skirts, shawls, saris, tablecloths and baby blankets. Issues of safety and hygiene were addressed too; we did not provide any head coverings to help prevent the spread of head lice.

Here are some materials useful in a home centre:

- child size furniture such as a stove, refrigerator, chair
- accessories found in the home (real items where possible), e.g., telephone, iron
- baby and toddler dolls representing different ages, sexes and races
- different sizes of clothes to fit the dolls. We provided inclusive, or multi-purpose, clothing of different sizes with different fasteners to provide natural opportunities for the children to develop their small muscle coordination and control. The clothing represented a variety of cultures, sexes and physical challenges
- real accessories for the dolls, e.g., baby bottles, bibs, rattles. We encouraged the children to bring other baby items from home to add to the selection.
- child size clothing for dress-up
- other real accessories, such as eyeglasses, jewelry, wallets
- adaptable items for dress-up, e.g., pieces of cloth, scarves
- models of food
- adaptable items to make their own models of food, e.g., playdough for spaghetti
- cooking utensils and dishes that represent a variety of cultures — woks, chopsticks, pasta bowls
- environmental print such as that found on food packages
- other print materials to extend the role play, e.g., cheque books, menus, message board, magnetic letters
- reading materials such as magazines, children's literature (narrative, expository, poetry), telephone books, recipe books, newspapers. We were careful to include reading materials at a variety of reading levels and in the different home languages of the children.

Materials That Extend the Learning in the Home Centre in a MAG Classroom

It was important for us to follow the interests and lead of the children when we were deciding what materials to add to the home centre. We found that extensions imposed by us were rarely as successful as those which occurred as a natural result of the children's dramatic play. In order to support the children's learning and to offer materials that would extend their interests and knowledge, we needed to visit the centre, interact with the children, and observe them carefully. After hearing a favorite story, such as The Three Billy Goats Gruff, the children often spontaneously transformed the home centre into a setting where they could re-enact portions of the story. They often used the big blocks and other props that we suggested to support their role playing.

Here are some examples of materials that can support extensions of the home centre. There is a wide range of extensions. The names of the most popular are asterisked.

OFFICES

Real Estate	home listings, for Sale and Sold signs, pads, pencils, business cards, briefcase, calculator, computer
*Veterinarian	pictures of pets, books about pets, cages, lost animal posters, prescription pads, stuffed animals, shampoo, labels from different pet foods, computer
*Doctor	eye chart, stethoscope, scales, plastic gloves, surgical gowns, bandages, crutches, appointment book, telephone
*Dentist	magazines, tooth chart, information on dental hygiene, instruments, plastic gloves, face mask, dental record cards, calculator
*Bank	blank cheques, deposit slips, bank books, signs, money, cash box, credit cards, tellers' wickets, calculators, adding machine

COMMUNITY STORES

Travel Agency	travel brochures, airline logos, paper, pencils, tickets, passports, visas, computer
Shoe Store	shoes, foot measurer, shoehorns, price labels, little mirrors, shoe polish, cash register, bills, boxes with different shoe sizes on them, bags from different shoe stores, adding machine, computer
*Restaurant	menus, cooking utensils, signs, aprons, dishes, trays, order pads, take-out containers, restaurant names, daily specials board, logos of familiar restaurants in the neighborhood, high chair
Gas Station	gas pumps, price signs, mechanic's tools, window washing equipment, different car brochures, safety glasses, heavy gloves, bills, clipboards, adding machine, calculators
*Hairdresser	combs, brushes and rollers (to use with the dolls, not each other), smocks, magazines, hair dryers, manicure tools, bills

EMERGENCY SERVICES

*Fire Station	sections of hose, heavy coats, plastic or cardboard hats, gloves, maps of the neighborhood, telephone numbers, cellular phone, paper, pencils, computer
Police Station	communication board with markers to show where different units are stationed, map of the area, handcuffs, badges, plastic hats, bulletproof vests, keys, flashlight, materials to write tickets, two-way radios
Radio or Television Station	microphones, commercial logos, lists of favorite shows, cameras, program guides, ad from local newspapers in first language as well as English, computer, fax machine, answering machine

OTHER SUCCESSFUL EXTENSIONS

Movie Theatre	advertisements, movie guide sections from various newspapers, flashlight, refreshment

	booth, familiar movie titles, empty video packages, book and tape sets, filmstrips and a little projector
Campsite	tent, sleeping bag, waterproof sheet to put sleeping bag on, water bottle, cooking utensils, knapsack, maps, compass, direction signs, names of campsites, travel brochures
*School or Daycare	art materials, building materials, reading materials, small easel with chalk, message board, writing materials, bell
*Airport, Train Station or Bus Station	money, blank tickets, materials to write tickets, departure and arrival schedule, steering wheel, earphones to listen to music or story tapes, food trays, newspapers, magazines, advertisements for other cities, names of stations or other destinations, luggage tags, suitcase rack

---

The Home Centre in a MAG Classroom: Some Questions for the Reflective Practitioner to Ask if an Environment for Success Is to Be Created

1. How do I ensure that the home centre remains inviting and organized?
   - You could add materials of good quality and discard broken or worn items.
   - You could allocate enough space for the children to have room to role-play.
   - Organize the home centre so that all materials have a place.
   - Select materials that represent the culture and family structures of the children in the class, e.g., children and single parent, children and grandparents.
   - Introduce additional materials that represent the broader community, e.g., paella pans.
   - Encourage the children to bring in materials from home to add to the centre.

- Involve the children when determining the number of children who can safely and productively use the centre.
- Continually review and modify the routines.

2. How do I ensure that the tidy up is successful and that it remains the responsibility of the children?
   - Carefully consider the centre's location and the traffic flow within the room. You will want to ensure that the centre is not disrupted and does not interfere with other centres in the room.
   - Carefully lay out the materials in an organized and labelled manner *before* the children are introduced to the centre.
   - Discuss new materials and establish new routines.
   - Give the children extra time so they can be responsible for the tidy up.
   - Ask other children to be monitors to check the centre after the tidy up.

3. How do I evaluate the children's role playing?
   - You could refer to the suggested mileposts to guide your observations. Remember that each child will not necessarily demonstrate all of the suggested mileposts.
   - Record how often the children voluntarily choose the centre.
   - Take note of the circumstances under which the children demonstrate the observed behaviors. Is it regularly? with teacher direction and support? rarely?
   - Take note of how well the children demonstrate the observed skills, knowledge or behavior. Do they do so reluctantly? confidently? enthusiastically? hesitantly?

4. How do I help to ensure that parents value the work in the home centre as much as work in the writing/drawing centre or reading corner?
   - You could share your knowledge and enthusiasm about the importance of providing opportunities for children to role-play.
   - You could demonstrate how much you value the centre by spending as much time adding to it, changing it, and talking about it as you do for a writing or interest centre.

- Schedule time to visit the centre.
- Regularly share your observations of the learning with the children and their parents. You might discuss conflict resolution, literacy, mathematical skills.
- On every occasion, including parents' night and in newsletters, take the opportunity to draw the parents' attention to the possible learning.
- Provide evidence of the children's learning in their portfolios and on bulletin boards. Use photographs, videos, tapes, and samples of their writing and reading.
- Encourage the parents to contribute materials for the centre.
- Invite parents to volunteer, for example, to help the children make real pizzas in the restaurant.
- Track the children's progress and share their development with the parents on a regular basis. You can use post-it notes and a page for each child.

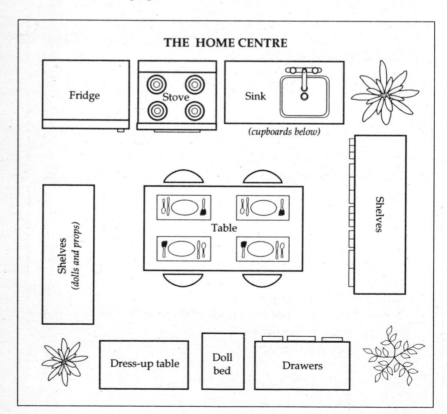

THE HOME CENTRE

Some Mileposts to Help Guide Teacher Observations of Children Working in the Home Centre in a MAG Classroom

The Ways That Children Role-play

They might:

___ watch other children role-play but remain uninvolved

___ work alone and ignore or remain oblivious to the other children

___ work near other children, using the same material but not become involved with the other children

___ work beside other children, sharing the equipment, experiences or ideas, but continue to be concerned with their own play and have little interest in what the other children are doing

___ work cooperatively with other children, sometimes assuming both leadership and follower roles

___ work collaboratively with other children, often planning and carrying out joint plans

The Behaviors That Children Demonstrate When They Role-play

They might:

___ assume familiar roles, e.g., mommy, daddy

___ assume imaginary roles, e.g., a princess

___ use familiar materials to support the role play, e.g., dolls

___ use new materials to support the role play, e.g., a calculator

___ share materials

___ create props from materials in the room, e.g., a firefighter's hat

___ take on different roles

___ solve problems. For example: "We can't both be the daddy, you be the uncle."

___ include others in the play

___ take turns

— show respect for others, such as by accepting their ideas

— follow routines, such as for tidy up

— show creative thinking and imagination

The Language Skills That Children Demonstrate When They Role-play

They might:

— use language to express their feelings and to sort out problems in new situations

— use language in appropriate contexts. For example: "I need a hose to put out the fire."

— use language for a variety of purposes, e.g., to retell, reflect, relate, direct, describe, question, inform

— use language in a variety of situations, including familiar and imaginary

— use reading and writing to support the role playing

The Ways That Children Show Their Interest in Role Playing

They might:

— choose to role-play

— willingly join in the role play when invited by the teacher or other classmates

— continue the role play over time

— bring items from home to support their role play

— ask the teacher, other classmates, parents and other visitors to be part of the role play

These developmental mileposts are guidelines only and are not intended to be all-inclusive or prescriptive.

12/Other Literacy Experiences

Primarily at the learning centres in the classroom, the children develop their abilities to think, communicate, problem-solve, and work cooperatively and collaboratively. However, other experiences are also important for the development of literacy in a MAG classroom. Additional learning activities such as personal reading times, read-aloud sessions, and shared writing times can be woven easily into the day. Sometimes, they occur before, during or at the end of the activity period.

Borrow-a-Book

The borrowing of books is an integral part of the literacy program in MAG classrooms. It helps to establish a concrete link between the home and the school in the important task of learning to read and write. Research shows that children who have been read to before arriving at school have a better chance for later academic success than those children who have not had such experiences. We believe the development of literacy is a shared responsibility, and so we spent time each day helping children to make selections of reading materials to share with their families.

We collected a wide range of reading materials that represented different cultures, physical abilities, races, gender roles and languages. Some titles are *Amazing Grace* by Rachel Isadora,

Cleversticks by Bernard Ashley, and *Mama Zooms* by Jane Cowen-Fletcher. We were careful to include materials, such as *Where's Spot?* by Eric Hill in Chinese, that both the children and their families could read. Sensitive to the home situations, we included wordless picture books for parents who might not be literate, first language materials for those families who could read only in a first language other than English, and materials that represented a variety of topics, cultures, genres, and levels of reading and listening ability.

We also encouraged the children to borrow reading materials that they could read to their family members. We had used these materials for instruction with the children and through this borrowing, they were able to practise, reinforce and demonstrate their learning to their families. We included a record card for the children and their family members to note the name of the book/tape/video borrowed, the date and their responses. Although we don't tend to view an audiotape or video as equivalent to a book, children do, so we allowed these story forms as well. *Rosie's Walk* by Pat Hutchins is a story that works equally well as a book, video and audiotape. We asked the families to comment in either their first language or English, and we took the time to reply to their comments.

Date	Title	Reader	Comment.
Oct 8/96	Ten in A Bed	Tony	(☺)
Oct 9/96	Just Like Daddy	sister - Amalia	she liked it.
Oct 11/96	Who's Afraid of the Dark	Mum	All o.k!
Oct 15/96	Bears, Bears Bears	Tony	I k nt
Oct 17/96	The Hungrey Cat	Tony	O.K
Oct 18/96	Amazing Grace	Mum	Beautiful Book!
Oct 21/96	Where the Wild Things Are	sister Amalia	Good story
Oct 24/96	There's a Monster in the Cbbt	sister Amalia	a bit scary
Oct 25/96	Where's Spot	Tony	Ez lot
Oct 29/96	Fly Homer Fly	Mum	We really enjoyed this book! Great message, great story. OK! Send more like this
Oct 30/96	Cloudland	Mum	I hope you like this story - its new - well, he really enjoyed it! May we have it again?

This Borrow-a-Book card indicates that a variety of family members did the reading.

110

This dialogue was very helpful in creating a fuller understanding of the children's interests, attitudes and skills in the acquisition of literacy.

To emphasize the program's value, we provided a special bag for carrying these materials home. The bag can be made of any sturdy material — waterproof cotton, linen or burlap. We personalized the bag only to the extent of identifying the school name and room number because we didn't want strangers to use name information to approach a child. This also allowed us to use the book bags from year to year. The bag needed to be big enough to carry a picture book. A size of 14 inches across by 16 inches deep works well.

Week of ___November 14–18___

	M	T	W	Th	F
			Borrows from Library →		
Tony					
Paul	Hide and Seek / Naughty Puppy / Monster hops	Wake up Charlie Dragon / Jump Frog Jump	Corduroy / When Panda Came to our house	Sam's Biscuit / Wilfred, Gordon. / Mr Donald Partridge	Dinosaurs ABC
Daniel		Snail Saves the Day	Arthur at Camp →	Three Little Kittens / A cat, fish & ...	
Heim Wah	Case of the Missing Dinosaur	Polar Bear Polar Bear	Chopsticks	Dinosaurs Encore. →	
George		Nicky's Picnic	Jolly Postman (Postman.) →		Willy the Wimp
Anna	Milton the Early Riser →		Arthur's Nose →		The Foundling
Sofia	Jellybean Fever	Bet You Can! / Rosie's Walk	→	Tigers / Amazing Grace →	
Johnson	Four Black Puppies / 10 Little Ducks	I Went Walking / Where the Wild Things Are →		Santa's Book of Names →	

Here, the teacher keeps track of children's reading choices.

We also kept accurate records of each child's choices. We did so in case the book card that went home got lost. Then we still had a record of who read what and when.

This program took considerable time and organization, but the benefits justified the extra effort. The children were eager to read and the parents appreciated the help the school offered in providing books and in making home reading more manageable. The program served also to help parents understand more about the process of learning to read and the critical nature of their role.

In MAG classrooms, the borrow-a-book experience is richer and more manageable than in traditional one-age/grade settings. The older children help the younger children make their choices, complete the borrowing cards and become familiar with the routines. The younger children quickly catch the enthusiasm of the more experienced borrowers. Also, the teacher has more time to help the more capable readers select more challenging materials and to make personal responses to parent comments or questions.

Shared Reading and Writing

Children need to have real reasons to read and write.

A Daily Message is one technique we used in our MAG classrooms to demonstrate authentic purposes. Such a message is short and provides the children with information about new activities or special events; for example, Today is gym day. Sometimes we wrote these messages with the children at the beginning or at the end of the day; for example, Tomorrow, remember to bring your permission form for the zoo trip.

The Daily Message technique can be used either as a shared reading or as a shared writing experience. That depends on whether or not the message is written with the children. During shared writing times, children learned new strategies, such as phonics, root words, vocabulary and punctuation, to assist them in their writing. During shared reading times, we introduced strategies to unlock unfamiliar words; these included re-reading and skipping and continuing.

We introduced many other kinds of shared reading experiences. We used big books and charts in order that a group of children could easily see the print. We included non-fiction, poetry, chants, songs and simple pattern books. These sessions allowed us to model specific reading strategies. We pointed out such features of the text as punctuation, spelling, grammar, the table of contents, and information about the author. We also used these times to have the children retell, demonstrate decoding strategies, and predict outcomes. Once the children were familiar with the text, we often created activities to reinforce the vocabulary; for example, adopting cloze procedure and framing individual words through the use of hands to isolate them.

The shared reading sessions provided opportunities for further literacy activities. We might create collaborative books based on the pattern in the original text, role-play familiar parts of the story, join in with the reading, create story maps, or construct vocabulary activities such as bingo, snap, and fish games.

Shared writing experiences provided authentic situations in which we could teach children how to write. By thinking out loud, we showed the children how writers write, how they compose, revise, and edit. "How can I say that?" "Where will I begin?" "That doesn't make sense." "I missed out a word." "Maybe I should move that sentence." We also demonstrated different writing forms. We taught the children how to write a letter or a poem, record a recipe, develop a table of contents and begin a fairy tale. We modelled different spelling strategies, such as phonics, root words and adding endings. We used these shared writing pieces for other children to read. We encouraged the children to include such writing in their home borrowing selections.

In traditional classroom settings the teacher often tends to use shared reading and writing activities with the whole class. However, motivating and meeting the needs of all the children at once is very difficult to do.

We found that these times were more meaningful and productive when we worked with small groups of children. We were better able to manage the groups and to ensure that all of the children were equally involved. Sometimes, we structured the groups so that the children were all of the same developmental level; at other times, we created groups for other reasons, such as interest or social. When the groups had different levels of reading and writing expertise, the more proficient readers and writers used vocabulary and strategies that the beginning readers and writers could note and imitate.

These times were richer than in homogeneous groupings because the children heard a variety of ideas, alternatives and suggestions. In MAG classrooms a wide range of competence and interest is present and these can be shared in order to facilitate literacy acquisition.

Personal Reading Time

We agree with Frank Smith when he says that children learn to read by reading. They need quality time to choose books that interest them, to enjoy the process of reading and to practise their skills. We scheduled a time each day for the children to select and read books of their own choice. We carefully established definite routines that ensured everyone would find this time productive. We insisted that the children read by themselves and not disturb others. We required the children to record their reading in a reading log.

We used this personal reading time effectively. We observed the children as they read or retold stories from the pictures or by memory. We noted book choices, the reading skills children used, the intensity of interest and their ability to concentrate. We also modelled our interest in reading by reading ourselves. We found doing this gave us a perfect opportunity to become familiar with new books from the library.

At the end of the personal reading time, children often spontaneously shared their enthusiasm or frustration with a particular book. Once again, because of the presence of the wider range of competent readers in the MAG classroom, children were exposed to different opinions, preferences, interests, authors, styles and titles. They shared ways to overcome frustrations: rereading a part, skipping parts, choosing another book. The more competent readers grew in confidence.

Reading Log – In School

Date	Title	Reader	Comment
Sept 24/96	Polar Bear Cat	Heim Wah and Matt.	- reads well - points to words - uses pictures
Sept 26/96	I Can Read	Heim Wah and Mimi	We read it 3 times. Its easy.
Oct 1/96	Four Black Puppies	Heim Wah and Matt.	- trying to use sounds. - relys on pattern - very confident.
Oct 3/96	How Do I Eat it	Heim Wah	(☺) Good
Oct 4/96	The Frog and the Fly	Heim Wah and Mimi	To easy. Mimi and Heim Wah - not this time try Just Like Daddy. Its harder!
Oct 8/96	A Dark Dark Tale	Heim Wah and Matt.	ready for step 2 a little further books?
Oct 11/96	Just Like Daddy	Heim Wah and Mimi	This was good. We hav nvr been fishing.
Oct 15/96	Piggies	Heim Wah and Mimi	Funny
Oct 18/96	Sam and the Lucky Money	Mr S.	a wonderful story. Illuminated me all about Lucky Money.

Buddy Reading and Writing

We recognized that children need many opportunities to read and write and practise their developing literacy skills.

Single-age and MAG classrooms approach this matter differently. In traditional single-age/grade classrooms, teachers often try to create more opportunities for support in reading and writing by twinning with an older class, that is, by introducing Buddy Reading. In MAG classrooms, creating these artificial conditions is unnecessary: there are many natural opportunities throughout the day for children to help each other or to accept help themselves.

In our MAG classrooms, we observed natural pairings of children and capitalized on these relationships. We often suggested that older children help specific younger children. The younger children, not being that far behind the older children, felt encouraged to read, believing they could catch up — if they had been teamed up with very proficient readers, they might have felt intimidated and assumed observers' roles. While helping the younger children or sharing their own work, the more proficient readers and writers had many opportunities to read and write for authentic purposes. The audience was always built in, and coaches were always available. Sometimes, one of the partners would be the coach, and on other occasions the other child would assume this role.

The children each had a designated partner to whom they could go for help and to share their own reading and writing. The children used their reading logs or writing folders to record these interactions. They noted the titles of the books shared, wrote comments about the reading materials and recorded any problems they encountered with the reading. They also added any specific suggestions that had been made about each other's writing.

Buddy reading and writing in a MAG classroom ensures that the feedback/response, that Cambourne insists is so critical in the acquisition of literacy, is always available.

Read-Aloud Sessions

When teachers take the time to read to children, they help to immerse children in the wonderful world of literature. They can introduce children to a variety of text, including poetic, expository, and narrative. By listening to stories read or told aloud, the children are motivated to read for themselves. They are introduced to real reasons for reading.

The selection of materials to be shared in read-aloud sessions is critically important. Sometimes, we invited the children to make selections to share with the class. However, we were careful to ensure that all the materials presented were inclusive and bias free. We made sure that the children in the room saw their own images and those of the broader community. One favorite was *Daniel's Dog* by Jo Ellen Bogart.

We read several times a day and used different materials for specific purposes. We used big books; for example, *Monster Mysteries*, to model specific text forms and introduce specific reading skills. We used simple pattern and repetitive text; for example, *I Went Walking*, so that children would be able to read these materials independently. Such materials also helped to motivate the children to use the patterns from the original text to create their own books: one might be *Mary Had a Red Dress*. We read lots of songs and chants which, after many group re-readings, the children were able to read on their own, *The Wheels on the Bus* being one. We selected stories such as *Rosie's Walk* because of their strong story line to help children retell and sequence events. We read the story to a significant point and then encouraged the children to predict what was going to happen next. *Wednesday's Surprise* was a good choice. We selected specific non-fiction materials to model the unique features of informational texts: table of contents, glossary, headings, charts, graphs and more. We also introduced the children to books that demonstrate a variety of techniques and illustrative materials, including flap books, pop-ups, and borders, in order to expand their use of illustrative techniques in their own writing and publishing. We also remembered to choose books that we enjoyed in order to promote infectious enthusiasm.

Many parents and educators question whether any read-aloud book can meet the interests, needs and levels of the varying ages in a MAG classroom. **We believe that stories are not written for any one reading level or age. Good literature appeals to children of all ages.** Many an adult enjoys a good children's story, such as *Charlotte's Web* by E.B. White. They do so with differing levels of understanding and enjoyment. The same is true for children in a MAG classroom. However, for the materials to appeal to children of all ages, the selection is critical. Picking any book off the shelf to read at the last minute is not enough to motivate or interest children, in any setting, MAG or otherwise.

We believe listeners of all ages need to have many experiences with the same book. Only by doing so can they read and listen beyond a literal level. Instead of becoming bored, the children are more enthusiastic about literature when they hear stories on several occasions. Each time we reread a familiar text, we offered different challenges and insights, so the children could see the value and purpose in rereading it. We might ask, "What might have happened if the giant had not wakened up?" If children and parents are to see the value in rereading, teachers must be explicit about why revisiting text is important.

Shared enjoyment could be one reason: "I just want to read this book again. It's so funny!" Through rereadings, children gain a deeper understanding of the author's message and listen at a more interpretive level. Encourage them to listen to more difficult text than they can read for themselves; they will then be motivated to choose more difficult text.

Read-aloud sessions can take place with the whole class or with a small group. In small group sessions the teacher or children can choose titles which suit particular interests and needs. *The Jolly Postman* is an excellent selection for children who are learning to write in role. In MAG classrooms, there are many opportunities for small group reading with the more proficient readers taking on the role of reader.

In conclusion, it is clear that MAG classrooms are best able to provide the conditions that Brian Cambourne has outlined as necessary for children to become successful readers and writers. Children of many ages are immersed in a rich literary environment, with easy-to-read picture books to simple chapter books. There are many readers and writers, in addition to the teacher, who can offer demonstrations and models of successful readers and writers. Children are expected to be and are successful in reading and writing. A variety of abilities and approximations are expected and accepted in the MAG classroom: scribble to chapter, memory reading to interpretive reading. There are many individuals who can offer positive responses and constructive feedback. For example: "You were smart to go back to the beginning when you couldn't figure out that one word." "Tell me what you are trying to say here. I'm confused." All children have time to practise and consolidate their skills in the company of other readers and writers. **In MAG classrooms the children have many natural opportunities to share in the responsibility of learning to read and write:** choice of titles/materials, of inquiries to follow, of topics to write about and of responses to make are some of these.

13/Key Questions Parents Ask About Multi-Age Groupings

1. **Are there advantages to putting children of different ages together?** *Yes*
   - The transition from home to school is made easier because new children enter a happy, secure, well-established learning environment.
   - New children have more models to imitate; e.g., readers, writers, problem solvers.
   - Younger children have other coaches beside the teacher to turn to for help.
   - The transition from grade to grade is less disruptive because children remain with the same teacher and peer group.
   - There is more time (two or three years) afforded to develop positive relationships: teacher and parents, teacher and children, children and children.
   - Older children know the routines and expectations of the teacher.
   - Older children have many opportunities to demonstrate their skills, knowledge and attitudes.
   - All children have more opportunities to act as both leaders and followers, to give and receive help, and to develop their confidence and self-esteem as learners.
   - The teacher's time is used more efficiently. The teacher has more time to teach due to routines and expectations

being firmly established with one-half to two-thirds of the children.

- Each year the teacher does not lose time becoming familiar with the individual abilities of a *whole* class of children.

2. **Don't the older children suffer academically because they are held back by the younger children?** *No*
   - Research indicates that there are no academic disadvantages for graduates of MAG programs.
   - MAG graduates achieve as well academically as those children who have been in traditional classroom settings.
   - Research has also shown that learners in MAG classrooms demonstrate higher levels of self-esteem, of a willingness to take risks, and of problem-solving abilities.
   - Teachers report that children appear more secure and confident and are more engaged in the learning process.
   - Teachers have an in-depth knowledge of the older children. As a result, they can offer a higher quality of challenge and expectation. They do not waste time at the beginning of each new academic year getting to know the capabilities and learning styles of the older children.

3. **Don't the younger children feel pressured by the presence of the older children?** *No*
   - Just as in a family setting, the youngest children feel reassured that many people are available to help, motivate and teach them.
   - The younger children gain confidence when they see how other children are succeeding with tasks that they feel are within their grasp. They adopt a positive attitude, thinking, "Soon I will be able to do that."
   - The younger children accept that there are many different levels of skill, interest and ability in all groups at home and school. They are very aware of their progress, often commenting, "I used to scribble like that, but now I make people with arms and legs."
   - We have never experienced children feeling inferior in our MAG classrooms because everyone was expected to perform according to his or her own ability.

- Our experience is that some children feel intimidated in traditional classroom settings where the only reader or writer, the teacher or another adult, is a very competent reader or writer.
- It has also been our experience that children are very aware of their abilities and rarely attempt activities that put them at risk; e.g., they do not climb up very high on a climber until they feel secure and confident at a lower level.
- Young children are very egocentric and mostly interested in what they can do, not what they can't do.

4. **Is it possible to provide quality instruction to children of different levels of ability?** *Yes*
   - Teachers have realized for many years that children learn best where the instruction is tailored to their needs. In MAG classrooms, teachers are not tempted to teach all of the children the same skills and knowledge at the same time.
   - Instruction is more effective and of a higher quality because the children are grouped according to interests and ability.
   - The broad range of capabilities affords more natural opportunities to group children.
   - MAG classrooms lend themselves to instruction in small groups. The children, because of their different ages, expect to work in groups and are more experienced in doing so.
   - Since children are with one teacher for a longer period of time, teachers are better able to match the instruction and learning activities to the children's individual capabilities and interests.
   - MAG teachers, because of the age range in their classrooms, become much more familiar with the developmental levels of instruction. This increased knowledge helps teachers to provide a higher quality of instruction.
   - Since the more competent children naturally adopt the role of coach and mentor, the other children get more individual help.

- Since teachers spend less time reinforcing routines and classroom expectations, they have more time to work with individual children and to plan appropriate programs.

5. **Is it more difficult to teach?** *No*
   - It is more difficult to teach only if the teacher holds narrow preconceived notions of what a particular age of children can do, think and value.
   - Successful MAG teachers focus on what the children know, do, and value and plan accordingly so that all of the children will experience success.
   - Teaching in traditional split-grade classrooms is harder because the teacher divides the learning into segments according to grade, not developmental level.
   - The emphasis in a MAG classroom is on continuous growth and process. Students of the same age are not expected to perform in the same manner or to produce the same product at the same time with the same level of success.
   - Teachers in MAG classrooms capitalize on the diversity of the children. Just as in a family, older children read to younger children, more competent children help learners tie their shoes, and so on.

6. **Do certain conditions determine whether multi-age grouping is beneficial for all children?** *Yes. These conditions are as follows:*
   - Parents understand and support the philosophy of MAG classrooms and are given input and choice regarding pupil placement.
   - Teachers understand the developmental nature of learning with young children.
   - Teachers want to work in a MAG organization.
   - Teachers are willing to reflect on their practices and to seek out more effective teaching strategies.
   - Administrators are knowledgeable about the benefits of a MAG organization and are supportive of its philosophy.
   - Staff are supportive of the long-range commitment necessary for successful MAG organizations.

7. **Can teachers deliver different grade-specific curriculum for each grade/age group?** *Yes*
   - Teachers plan by grade division to ensure there will be no repetition of curricular content.
   - Teachers in MAG classrooms realize that a topic is never really repeated since the children work at varying levels of understanding and complexity and follow different paths of inquiry.
   - With young children, the curricular emphasis in all classrooms should be on communication, inquiry, data management and problem solving. The specifics of the content vary according to the developmental levels and interests of the children.
   - Grade-specific content is easily and more meaningfully incorporated into small group investigations; read-aloud times; shared reading and writing opportunities; listening, viewing, and discussion sessions; and other integrated learning opportunities. For example: If all six-year-olds must study magnets, teachers can choose to have them read about magnets or write about them. Or, they could incorporate students' learning into the math/science/technology activities in more natural and meaningful ways that capitalize on the multi-age group's rich and varied experiences.
   - In activities such as physical education, teachers are careful to ensure that the children use the apparatus in a variety of ways; e.g., all children are not expected to demonstrate the same ball handling skills. The teacher offers an open-ended challenge. For example: "Move the ball around the room." Some children might roll the ball, others might carry it, and others could bounce it.

8. **Is there duplication for the older children?** *No*
   - Content learning and the acquisition of skills in many subject areas in MAG classrooms are not simply repeated but rather they are introduced or extended. For example: With young children the topic Animal Habitats might be confined to a particular group of animals (pets), while children who have some understanding of the topic may

investigate the habitats of wild, domestic or farm animals.

- Each time learners of all ages encounter a similar topic, they do so with a more complex level of understanding, building on what they already know.
- In skills such as reading and writing, children don't simply duplicate or repeat their already achieved skills. Instead, they continue to build on these skills and to develop new competencies.
- All learners gain from sharing their knowledge and skills with others; e.g., even though children might know how to add and subtract to 10, they gain confidence in their own learning as they share this skill with less competent learners.
- Although parents may worry about the older children in a MAG classroom being held back, the reality is that they do not copy what the younger children do; rather, they take pride in acquiring new skills and knowledge that they can share with their classmates.
- MAG teachers expect children not to duplicate their learning. They plan activities and learning experiences that will challenge all the children.

9. **Is it difficult for Grade 1 children to cope with two different sets of Kindergarten children (morning and afternoon) and the possible repetition of learning experiences?** *No*
   - Teachers in Kindergarten plan learning activities, make different selections of songs and stories and create interest centres to meet the needs and interests of the two groups.
   - In the event that a story or learning experience is repeated, all learners benefit as they bring differing experiences, insights and understandings to the repeated experience. For example: Hearing a story for a second time helps children to retell with more competence and confidence. They add more details and more accurately sequence events.
   - If teachers are concerned about the value of a repeated experience, they can direct children to other activities.

The children could complete an activity begun in the morning or begin a new independent inquiry.
- The children who come to school all day have more choice and opportunity to form social relationships.

10. **Do the children have to stay in the MAG classroom if a personality conflict arises between the teacher and the child or other children?** *No*
    - Pupil placement procedures are no different than those in traditional classrooms. The best interests of the children are always a priority.
    - If a conflict arises, teachers and parents discuss the problem with the administration and develop a plan that addresses it.
    - If the personality conflict persists, staff and parents need to consider a change in placement, weighing all the factors involved.
    - Children would not be forced to remain in a MAG classroom where the parents/guardians did not support the placement.

Conclusion

We believe that MAG classrooms are more successful in serving the learning needs of young children for several reasons. They reflect the very best of the real-life learning opportunities present in a family. They provide a natural, supportive learning environment for young children. With the increased consistency, stability, and security, they ensure a less stressful, early childhood school experience. They create a cooperative and collaborative climate as opposed to one of competition. With the extra time and opportunities, students become more confident in themselves as learners. We believe MAG classrooms provide a more humane approach to education, where the focus is on the child as a learner rather than on arbitrarily assigned expectations according to age or grade.

As MAG teachers, we felt that our work was validated. We saw the children's tremendous growth in knowledge, skills and attitudes over the two- or three-year period that they were with us. We recognized that we had made a difference in the lives of the children and their families. With a more in-depth knowledge of all of the children, their interests, needs and abilities, we were able to provide for continuous, uninterrupted growth and learning. The extra time of the MAG structure allowed us to evaluate continuously, making better use of authentic assessment strategies such as portfolios, cumulative tracking sheets, student and parent evaluations, and student-led conferences. There was no need to consider failure, grade repetition or fast-tracking. Because individual differences were expected and celebrated, the children respected and valued diversity. They lived and learned in an atmosphere that was naturally inclusive of all abilities, ages and interests. These experiences supported them in developing a mind set which provided a foundation for an understanding of the importance of equity. Fewer discipline problems emerged since the children had formed such close relationships, learned to understand their differences and engaged more actively in their learning. The children worked in harmony and became responsible, self-sufficient and confident learners. They had many opportunities to learn how to lead and to follow, to learn and to teach in a variety of situations.

We believe that we established a closer rapport and partnership with parents. These parents became more involved in their children's learning at school and at home. As they came to a deeper understanding about education today, they became strong advocates for MAG classrooms. They also became stronger supporters of the public education system.

Clearly, given the choice, we would *never* elect to teach in any setting other than a multi-age grouping.

Index

reading log, 114, 115, 116
relationship,
    children & children, 18,
        19, 20, 21, 25, 39, 49,
        115-16, 127
    children & teacher, 21
    teacher and children's
        families, 21-22, 127
responsibility for learning,
    15, 26, 28, 84, 109, 127
risk taking, 17-18, 20, 29, 37,
    38, 89, 99
routines,
    importance of, 32, 114-15
    introduction of, 21, 23, 25,
        32, 55
    questions to consider
        when developing, 33

sand centre, 69-74
    materials that encourage
        learning, 70-71
    mileposts to guide teacher
        observations, 73-74
    questions for the
        reflective practitioner to
        ask, 71-72
    why needed, 69-70
self-confidence, 17-18, 19, 89,
    99, 122
single-age classrooms. *See*
    MAG classrooms.
skills, knowledge and
    attitudes, 17, 18-19, 29, 69,
    82, 83, 84, 100, 126
Smith, Frank, 114
split grades, 9, 12

teachers,
    in MAG classrooms, 14-15,
        18, 19, 25, 38-39

    in single-age classrooms,
        12, 16, 18, 20, 29, 36-37,
        76, 83, 92, 113
time,
    efficient use of, 23-24
    necessary, 12, 15, 20-23,
        33-34
timetables,
    achieving a manageable
        focus, 33-34
    effective, 32-33
    sample, 35

visual arts centre, 36-47
    materials that encourage
        make-it activities, 40
    materials that encourage
        modelling, 41-42
    materials that encourage
        painting, 39
    mileposts to guide teacher
        observations, 45-47
    questions for the
        reflective practitioner to
        ask, 43-44
    why needed, 36

water centre, 75-81
    materials that encourage
        learning, 77
    mileposts to guide teacher
        observations, 80-81
    questions for the
        reflective practitioner to
        ask, 78-79
    why needed, 75-76
writing/drawing centre. *See*
    drawing/writing centre.